EUL VERLAG

QUANTITATIVE ÖKONOMIE

Herausgegeben von Prof. Dr. Eckart Bomsdorf, Köln, Prof. Dr. Wim Kösters, Bochum, und Prof. Dr. Winfried Matthes, Wuppertal

Band 151
Ralf G. Gerhardt
Analyse des Kraftstoff- und Shop-Geschäfts des Tankstellennetzes einer Mineralölgesellschaft mit Hilfe von Regressionsverfahren
Lohmar – Köln 2007 • 152 S. • € 42,- (D) • ISBN 978-3-89936-606-8

Band 152
Jan Bottermann
Der transatlantische Realzinsverbund – Eine Untersuchung des US-Einflusses auf die deutsche Zinsstrukturkurve
Lohmar – Köln 2008 • 222 S. • € 45,- (D) • ISBN 978-3-89936-690-7

Band 153
Alexandra Schwarz
Lokale Scoring-Modelle
Lohmar – Köln 2008 • 248 S. • € 46,- (D) • ISBN 978-3-89936-725-6

Band 154
Andreas Nastansky
Realwirtschaftliche Folgen von Vermögenspreisschwankungen – Eine Kointegrationsanalyse für die Bundesrepublik Deutschland
Lohmar – Köln 2008 • 248 S. • € 56,- (D) • ISBN 978-3-89936-741-6

Band 155
Ronald Franken
Support-Vektor-Maschinen und statistische neuronale Netze im Data Mining und Datenqualitätsmanagement – Eine empirische Analyse am Beispiel der Unternehmenssolvenz
Lohmar – Köln 2008 • 348 S. • € 63,- (D) • ISBN 978-3-89936-756-0

Band 156
Dana Schüler
Macroeconomic and Microeconomic Effects of Migration
Lohmar – Köln 2009 • 236 S. • € 56,- (D) • ISBN 978-3-89936-769-0

JOSEF EUL VERLAG

On the Macroeconomic and Microeconomic Effects of Migration

Dissertation zur Erlangung des wirtschaftswissenschaftlichen Doktorgrades der Wirtschaftswissenschaftlichen Fakultät der Universität Göttingen

vorgelegt am 14. Jul. 2008
von Dana Schüler
geboren am 8. Nov. 1978
in Dresden, Deutschland

Erstgutachter: Prof. Stephan Klasen, PhD.

Zweitgutachter: Prof. Andy McKay, PhD.

Datum der Disputation: 11. Okt. 2008

Reihe: Quantitative Ökonomie · Band 156

Herausgegeben von Prof. Dr. Eckart Bomsdorf, Köln, Prof. Dr. Wim Kösters, Bochum, und Prof. Dr. Winfried Matthes, Wuppertal

Dr. Dana Schüler

Macroeconomic and Microeconomic Effects of Migration

EUL VERLAG

Bibliographische Information der Deutschen Bibliothek

Die Deutsche Bibliothek verzeichnet diese Publikation in der Deutschen Nationalbibliothek; detaillierte bibliographische Daten sind im Internet über <http://dnb.ddb.de> abrufbar.

Dissertation, Universität Göttingen, 2008, unter dem Titel: On the Macroeconomic and Microeconomic Effects of Migration

ISBN 978-3-89936-769-0
1. Auflage Februar 2009

JOSEF EUL VERLAG GmbH
Brandsberg 6
53797 Lohmar
Tel.: 0 22 05 / 90 10 6-6
Fax: 0 22 05 / 90 10 6-88
http://www.eul-verlag.de
info@eul-verlag.de

Bei der Herstellung unserer Bücher möchten wir die Umwelt schonen. Dieses Buch ist daher auf säurefreiem, 100% chlorfrei gebleichtem, alterungsbeständigem Papier nach DIN 6738 gedruckt.

Acknowledgment

I am very grateful to my advisor, Stephan Klasen, for the helpful discussions on several papers. Without him this thesis would not have been possible. I would also like to thank the members of my committee, Andy McKay and Walter Zucchini, for their advice and time. I am indebted to Jann Lay who provided the Ghanaian household data and incorporated me in the research project "Rural Poverty and Distributional Change in sub-Saharan Africa". Furthermore, I would like to thank my colleagues at the University of Göttingen for their cooperation and friendship. Lastly, I am indebted to the most important people in my life, my family and friends.

Dana Schüler

Göttingen, den 10. Jul. 2008

Contents

List of Figures

List of Tables

General Introduction and Main Findings

The topic that connects all three studies of this dissertation is migration. Therefore the first part of this dissertation embeds the studies in the recent literature on migration. Nevertheless, the individual chapters are not only about migration. This is described in detail below.

Internal and international migration flows become increasingly important in the process of global integration. One of the most frequent forms of diversification is migration. Migration has quite different shapes and underlying motivations. Notwithstanding these differences, the central reason for migration is the attempt to secure a better standard of living.

Almost everywhere internal migration is more important than international migration. Deshingkar and Grimm (2004) summarize the findings of several studies, from India and Vietnam for instance, which show that internal migration is much more important than international migration. The ongoing importance of internal migration can be explained by a growth process concentrated in urban areas, structural adjustment programs that made diversification of income-portfolios necessary, population pressure, and growing competition on globalized markets that led to a reduction in prices for agricultural products. International migration is most likely driven by the significant gap in earnings and welfare between countries.

A further important differentiation of migration arises from the duration of migration. Migration may be short-term or long-term. Both of these types can be driven by the pull factor of better opportunities in urban or other rural areas or countries. Short-term migration often results from the need to diversify out of agriculture due to the seasonality of farm work. In economically and infrastructure-weak regions individuals might be especially pushed into permanent (e)migration. As will be shown in this analysis, and as has been shown by Acemoglu (2001), the time-horizon of migrants can be a decisive determinant of the impact of migration. International migrants or "settlers" with a long-term perspective - if successful - might launch growth-enhancing long-term investments in the host country. Münz et al. (2006) highlight that economic effects depend on the skills of migrants.

Migration flows have a quite distinct impact on the recipient and the sending country. Some of the most important effects shall be analysed more deeply in this study. Firstly, a short review of the most important findings of the other strands of the literature is presented.

The second chapter, based on joint work with Julian Weisbrod, of this paper deals with the effects of migration on recipient countries. A wide range of literature analyses the short-run and long-run consequences of immigration on growth of the host country. Whether the effect is beneficial depends on whether migrant skills are complementary in the host country's labour market (OECD, 2003; OECD, 2007). Even low-skilled migrants can therefore be beneficial to the host country. Furthermore Borjas (1995) argues that migrants in general generate an immigration surplus by increasing the domestic GDP and possibly reducing production costs. The theoretical growth literature on the other hand considers the impact of migrants on the stock of human capital in the host country. Barro and Sala-i-Martin (1995) stressed the fact that migrants might increase the stock of human capital. The neoclassical growth theory predicts that the positive long-run growth effect of immigration depends on whether the capital per capita (financial and human) migrants are endowed with is higher relative to that of the host country's population. Walz (2001) reasons that endogenous growth theory predicts that only highly skilled migrants are beneficial although this leads to a brain drain in the sending country. Empirical evidence for European countries shows that highly skilled migrants are complementary to investment and therefore especially beneficial for economic development (Münz et al., 2006).

Reviewing who migrates suggests that relatively more high-skilled migrants are attracted by Northern America whereas relatively more low-skilled migrants enter Europe (OECD, 2007). This is largely driven by differences in migration policies. Deshingkar and Grimm's (2004) review of internal migration studies shows also that the highly-skilled are not necessarily likelier to migrate. The poorest (in terms of financial and skill endowments) households are not able to migrate because they do not have enough financial and labour resources.

A further aspect of migration is that immigration leads to more cultural diversity and might lead to significantly higher ethnic diversity in the host country. On the one hand, there are numerous studies in which it is argued that high ethnic diversity is detrimental to growth and is one of the key factors explaining the adverse growth experiences in many countries and regions. On the other hand, the literature on co-ethnic networks argues and gives evidence that immigrants build networks that facilitate trade and foreign direct investment. Furthermore, Acemoglu (2001) argued that settlers with a long-term perspective in recipient countries build institutions resembling those in the sending countries that enable investment and growth in the future. Furthermore, Lazear (1999) shows that diversity can increase productivity. This effect arises because workers with different cultural backgrounds and skills are complementary. This study has the aim of bringing together these different strands of the literature.

The second chapter reviews the studies that have found robust evidence for the negative effect of high ethnic fractionalisation on long-run growth in a cross section of countries (Easterly and Levine (1997), Easterly (2001), Alesina et al. (2003)). The channels through which ethnic fractionalisation has a negative impact on growth, however, have been analysed only partially by these studies. Furthermore, the impact of ethnic fractionalisation on economic progress is far more complex than the existing empirical research would suggest. For this reason this study extends the existing analysis in two ways.

First of all, the robustness of the model and transmission channels of ethnic fractionalisation on growth specified by Alesina et al. (2003) is checked by focusing on specific regions and by including the 1990s. The empirical results indicate that there is a 1990s and Sub-Saharan African effect of ethnic fractionalisation which cannot be explained by the Alesina et al. model. In the 1990s specifically, ethnic fractionalisation seems to have an effect on growth through influencing governance negatively. Governance seems to have gained importance in that decade. In Sub-Sahara Africa specifically, ethnic fractionalisation has an effect on growth via investment. This is in line with the argument of Walz (2001) who hypothesises that ethnic diversity could lead to less savings in a society. Secondly, we empirically investigate, if ethnic fractionalisation might have a mitigating positive impact in a nation which is ethnically diverse partially due to past immigration. There is a large literature which suggests that the existence of co-ethnic networks has a significant stimulating impact on trade and foreign direct investment and thus growth. The theoretical argument is that immigrants have an informational and trust advantage in arranging trade with their home countries over their local counterparts (Epstein and Gang, 2004; Casella and Rauch, 1997; Rauch, 2001; Tong, 2005). Several studies give evidence on the growth-enhancing effect of trade (Levine and Renelt, 1992; Frankel and Romer, 1999; Acemoglu, 2005) and openness (Ades and Glaeser, 1999). Inbound foreign direct investments are found to be complementary to domestic investment (Feldstein, 1994; Desai et al., 2005). The measure of ethnic fractionalisation, which is based on data of group shares listed in the Encyclopaedia Britannica (2001), allows to put the analysis in the context of the findings by Acemoglu (2001). Long-term immigrants help in building institutions that are beneficial to investment. In contrast, due to the measure of ethnic fractionalisiation, the analysis finds no evidence for the trade and foreign direct investment channel.

The analysis shows that the effects of ethnic diversity on growth are complex and one has to be careful in taking the pessimistic view of most existing authors who have written on the topic. Ethnic diversity as such might not be detrimental to economic growth. Politicians and media, however, can influence people's perceptions of differences between groups and therefore increase polarization. The theoretical arguments that demonstrate the negative growth effect depend decisively on the assumption of a polarization of interests and opinions as well as the segregation of different groups and high inequality between these groups in the society. These differences exist between different ethnic but also social groups of a society. Therefore it cannot be concluded that the ethnic and not the social divide is the real core of the problem. This means that ethnic diversity will become "a problem" if media and politicians adopt a rhetoric that overemphasises differences between ethnic groups and thereby fuel conflicts. Recent history in African countries like Rwanda and Kenya has shown that potentates or oppositional groups can misuse an apparent ethnic divide to strengthen their own power.

The last two chapters are devoted to the study of effects of migration on the sending country or region. Several aspects have to be highlighted before turning to the themes specifically analysed in this study. In the last years the focus of analysis has shifted away from the emphasis on the negative consequences of migration to a more technical analysis of how sending countries can profit from, and influence migration.

A recent publication of the OECD (2007) emphasises that the impact of migration depends on the phase of the "life cycle of migration" in which a sending country is situated. The first phase can be characterized by the "exit" of migrants. The exact macro-economic effects on the sending country depend on the skills of migrants and the size of emigration. If the relatively skilled leave the country the brain drain will hurt the country's economy through a reduction in the country's productivity. A country's production can also be reduced through a large net emigration of relatively unskilled laborers. Furthermore, net emigration has social consequences. The operation of a social security system - be it formal or informal - is troubled when the elderly are left behind. In the next phases these migrants will send remittances. Resource flows will increase further with the forming of migration networks. The welfare and growth effect of remittances are two quite distinct fields of research here. On the welfare side and at the micro-level it can be said that remittances might be an effective insurance and diversification instrument for the recipient household. The covariance of shocks experienced by the migrant and household of origin can be lowered if the migrant emigrates to a different region or country compared to the place of residence of the household. The insuring character of remittances can be attributed to internal as well as international transfer flows (Chapter 2; Chapter 3; Wolff et al., 2007; World Bank, 2007; Azam and Gubert, 2005). Furthermore, remittances are found to be positively correlated with expenditure (Boayke-Yiadom and McKay, 2007; Adams, 2007; Andersen and Tejerina, 2005). Whether remittances have a poverty-reducing effect depends on which households receive the transfers - the relatively poor or the relatively rich. The poverty reducing effect of remittances is found to be small (Adams, 2006). Andersen and Tejerina (2005) find evidence that remittances are positively related to an increase in health expenditure in Nicaragua.

Furthermore, in the face of credit market imperfections in developing countries, remittances might loosen the credit market constraint and facilitate investment (Woodruff, 2001). But investment opportunities might be missing due to a lack of infrastructure (Hugo, 2005).

These potential positive impacts on welfare and growth, however, can be rendered insignificant. Possible negative effects of remittances comprise a Dutch Disease effect at the macroeconomic level as wells as detrimental behavioral responses at the microeconomic level.

The Dutch Disease effect is said to arise due to the massive inflow of foreign exchange. If this money is spent on domestic products, inflation that leads to a real appreciation of the currency could hurt the economy. Moreover, if the recipients spent the money on non-tradeable goods the economy could shift towards non-traded goods production (OECD, 2007). However, a recent analysis of Rajan and Subramanian (2005) cannot confirm that remittances diminish competitiveness.

The third chapter of this study analyses the behavioral response of remittances on the recipient household. The shape of the behavioral response is central for assessing whether a poverty reducing and a macroeconomic Dutch Disease effect possibly exist. If remittances are used as a substitute for other income, expenditure won't rise and thus poverty and inflation are unaffected. In other words, the behavioral response determines the crowding-out of these effects.

The analysis differs from earlier studies reconsidering incentive effects on the labor market in that it examines whether there exist adverse incentive effects of transfers on working hours rather than on labor market participation of the working age population. The theoretical framework can be described shortly. The disincentive is generated by the informational asymmetries that exist between the migrant and the household of origin. Transfers cause a positive income effect. As a result, if leisure is considered a normal good, more leisure will be consumed. However, it might be that the stream of transfers an individual receives over time is incentive-compatible in that transfers do not react to all changes in income perfectly. In other words, if transfers do not provide perfect insurance, the disincentive is clearly reduced. Due to informational asymmetries, the effort level of recipients to avoid the event of a shock can only be observed imperfectly. An incentive compatible contract is not possible. Furthermore, the informational asymmetry between migrants and household members left behind makes it impossible to evaluate whether the recipient supplemented the insurance provided through the family network with formal or other informal insurance.

The empirical results for Indonesia indicate that there is a negative incentive effect on work effort, especially in the informal sector. The study differentiates between sectors since the expected effects vary substantial between them. This has not been analysed before. First of all, the formal and the informal labor market are analysed separately. This is based on the fact that formal sector workers are less flexible in adjusting their working hours, and that the costs of doing so might be higher for them. Furthermore, there is the possibility of oppositional effects of transfers between sectors. Whether an individual works mainly in the subsistence agricultural or the non-agricultural sector has major implications for the impact of transfers. Migrants may restrict household production since missing labor is difficult to replace in the agricultural sector (Rozelle, 1999). Furthermore, in rural areas credit market constraints might be more severe. Transfers may relax this constraint, enabling households to invest in more productive assets. Rural areas, however, also face missing opportunities of non-farm engagement. Therefore it is unclear whether remittances can give the incentive to start working in the non-farm sector. More importantly, the relaxation of the credit constraint might lead to investment in better technology. This clarifies that a focus on working hours might be flawed. In the agricultural sector disincentive effects should instead be measured by investigating a potential reduction in productivity of the farm household.[1]

The last phase in the life cycle of migration considers the return of migrants. In this return phase the country's economy can especially profit. This is because migrants usually tend to invest their savings (Deshingkar and Grimm, 2004). Kilic et al. (2007), for example, finds evidence that households with past migrants are more likely to own a non-farm enter-

1 A negative sign of the variable "transfers" may more realistically imply the substitution of labor by more productive assets.

prise in Albania. This holds true for the period of 1990-2000, but not for period of 2000-2004.

The Chapter 4, based on joint work with Jann Lay, has again a more general view on migration. It does so from the perspective of diversification strategies. In countries which are characterized by large economic differences within a country, which is the case in developing countries and emerging market economies, migration is one of the key household strategies to adjust in the process of development and reap some of the fruits of economic change. This chapter shows that migration essentially characterizes the process of structural change.

A wide range of literature has shown that the income portfolio of rural households comprises quite different sources. Diversification can take the form of non-farm sector participation in the form of self- or wage employment or migration of a part of household members. Migration, however, is often by far the most frequent form of diversification (Chapter 4). In order to specify the welfare consequences of increased diversification it is important to analyse the motivation behind it. Most likely, poor households diversify out of desperation. If diversification is mainly desperation-led, growth in remittances or the non-farm sector might be pro-poor. This, however, can lead to vicious cycles of low returns and low productivity in the farm sector and therefore to enduring poverty. If on the other hand diversification is opportunity-led and concentrated among the asset-rich, poor households might face severe entry constraints that prevent them from reaping the benefits of a prosperous economic development.

The empirical results demonstrate that rural household in Ghana indeed increasingly diversify their livelihoods by both increased migration and more local non-farm employment. Yet, only asset-rich households seem to be successful diversifiers. Poorer households increase the income share in particular from local non-farm activities through more participation while returns to diversifying activities stagnate or even decrease. In this sense, diversification appears to be driven to a large extent by desperation and asset-poor households increasingly diversify and remain poor.

Furthermore, the empirical analysis discloses non-negligible signs of structural change at the microeconomic level in Ghana though macroeconomic data suggest that no structural transformation took place between 1991 and 1998. Households significantly withdraw labour from the farm sector to increasingly engage in migration and the local non-farm sector. Chapter 4 further analyses the poverty and inequality consequences of these changes in diversification behavior in Ghana between 1991 and 1998.

This dissertation is structured as follows. Chapter 2 analyses the macro-economic consequences of past settlement via increased ethnic diversity on growth in the recipient country. The following two chapters are devoted to the analysis of the impact of migration on the sending country. Chapter 3 analyses whether remittances generate an adverse behavioral response on work effort, thereby crowding out possible positive, but also negative effects on development. Chapter 4 investigates whether migration is an important household diversification strategy and determines the consequences of increased diversification on poverty and inequality. The empirical analysis of Chapter 3 and 4 relies on micro data of Indonesia and Ghana.

Chapter 1

Ethnic Fractionalisation, Migration and Growth

1.1 Introduction

A wide range of studies have found robust evidence for the negative effect of high ethnic fractionalisation on long-run growth in a cross section of countries. This growth diminishing effect of ethnic fractionalisation has been found to be operating through an adverse policy environment and the suboptimal provision of public goods (Easterly and Levine (1997), Easterly (2001), Alesina et al. (2003)). However, the channels through which ethnic fractionalisation has an impact on growth have been analysed only partially by these studies. Furthermore, the impact of ethnic fractionalisation on economic progress might be far more complex than the existing empirical studies would suggest. For this reason this paper intends to extend the existing analyses.

First of all, it seems reasonable and desirable to update the data set used by Alesina et al.(2003) into the 1990s to analyse the robustness of

This chapter is based on joint work with Julian Weisbrod.

their results in a wider time range. Interestingly, we find a prevailing negative direct effect of ethnic fractionalisation on growth after the inclusion of the 1990s, despite the inclusion of policy control variables. Hence, we apply decade- and region-specific regressions, as well as a region-specific ethnic fractionalisation interaction term, in order to identify whether this result is driven by decade- or region-specific effects. We find that the growth hampering impact of ethnic fractionalisation remains in the 1990s and in Sub-Saharan Africa once the policy framework of Alesina et al. (2003) is controlled for. Moreover, we show that this 1990s effect vanishes if we implement the Kaufman-Kraay-Zoido-Lobaton-Indicator of governance in the existing model framework of Alesina et al.. The specific Sub-Saharan effect of fractionalisation shows an indirect effect via investment on growth. This is consistent with the argumentation of Walz (2001) presented below who hypothesises that natives do only care about fellow ethnic group members and therefore save less if they fear that another group could get stronger in size as well as power. In line with recent research on violent conflict (Montalvo and Reynal-Querol, 2005), we cannot confirm the hypothesis that the remaining negative impact of ethnic fractionalisation is due to violent conflicts. Thus, our results indicate that the original model specification of Alesina et al. is incomplete as it fails to fully account for the recent 1990s and Sub-Saharan growth experience.

In addition, it might be the case that the alleged negative effect of ethnic fractionalisation on growth, described above, is possibly mitigated by positive effects prevailing in multi-ethnic societies. Lazear (1999) shows that diversity can increase productivity. This effect arises because workers with different cultural backgrounds and skills are complementary. Furthermore, there is a large body of literature which suggests that the existence of co-ethnic networks has a large positive impact on trade and thus on growth. The theoretical argument is that immigrants have an informational and trust advantage in arranging trade with their home countries over their local counterparts (Epstein and Gang (2004), Casella and Rauch (1997), Rauch (2001)). Co-ethnic networks are also found to promote foreign direct investment in the host country (Tong, 2005). Several studies give evidence on the growth-enhancing effect of trade (Levine and Renelt, 1992; Frankel and Romer, 1999; Acemoglu, 2005) and openness (Ades and Glaeser, 1999). Inbound foreign direct investments are found to be complementary to domestic investment (Feldstein, 1994; Desai et al., 2005). Hence, we empirically investigate, whether the growth effect of ethnic fractionalisation might be positive in a nation which is ethnically diverse according to our indicator, partially due to past immigration. We find some indication that countries which are ethnically diverse due to past immigration can partly mitigate the negative impact of ethnic fractionalisation on growth. We are the first, to our knowledge, to distinguish between these two different kinds of ethnic fractionalisation in order to determine whether the result empirically indicates this multidimensionality of ethnic diversity. We find the positive effect but we cannot confirm the trade and foreign direct investment hypothesis. In fact ethnic diversity in immigrant countries seems to foster investment. This is in line with the argument of Acemoglu (2001) who demonstrated the positive effect of past settlement on institution building and thus long-run growth.

This chapter is structured as follows: In the 2nd and 3rd section of this chapter we will focus on the existing theoretical consideration and empirical research which has been produced so far. This is followed by a brief discussion of our data and methodology in section 1.4. Then we shall present and discuss our results in section 1.5. In section 1.6 we identify potentially interesting future research questions and conclude.

1.2 Theoretical Framework

There are two different strands of literature, one of which suggests that ethnic diversity is harmful to growth and another which suggests the opposite.

Zak and Knack (2001), for instance, argue that high ethnic diversity increases the social distance between groups, which in turn reduces the amount of trust in a society. Due to the significant information and enforcement problems in many (particularly risky) economic transactions, lack of trust will reduce the amount of beneficial economic transactions, increase transaction costs on monitoring and enforcement and will make some contracts impossible. A related insight emerges from the literature on 'social capital' which measures the number and intensity of social interactions and linkages between members of a society and has found that social capital is potentially conducive to economic development because it favours cooperation and reduces problems due to asymmetric information. The theoretical argument is that social capital is harder to establish between divided ethnic groups in a society. However, the theoretical literature on social capital also suggest that social capital can slow down the transition process of development between one stage and the next and can therefore be bad for economic growth (Banerjee and Newman, 1998; Arnott and Stiglitz, 1991)

Furthermore, some authors argue that ethnic diversity increases the likelihood of conflict. Collier and Hoeffler (1998) model the likelihood of a civil war as a cost-benefit calculation of potential rebels. While ethnic diversity is likely to increase the incentive to incite rebellion due to grievances (perceived and actual) experienced by individual ethnic groups, having very large numbers of ethnic groups might make the co-ordination of a successful rebellion difficult. Thus, Collier and Hoeffler argue that civil wars are particularly likely in ethnically polarised societies, where a few ethnic groups vie for political control.

Hence, not only violent, but also political conflict has been hypothesised as a channel through which high ethnic diversity negatively influences economic growth. Alesina and Drazen (1991) suggest that groups may attempt to shift the burden of economic stabilisation and reform onto other groups when stabilisation has significant distributional implications. Even though it is agreed that stabilisation requires cuts in public expenditure to eliminate the budget deficit, the distribution of the allocation of the costs is not agreed upon. The process leading to stabilisation might therefore be described as a war of attrition, which delays stabilisation and only ends when certain groups allow the others to decide on the allocation of the burden of the fiscal adjustment. More politically polarised countries will experience longer periods of instability. In the case that different ethnic groups are also strongly politically polarised then the model also applies in the context of ethnic diversity. Similar arguments are made by Easterly and Levine (1997), who argue that high ethnic diversity leads to poor policy choices. Governments either find it difficult to agree on painful economic reforms, attempt to shift the burden to other groups, or simply try to enrich themselves as they fear that their tenure might be limited due to the strong resistance of other ethnic groups. Svensson (1998) develops a game-theoretic, rent-seeking model in which groups compete for common-pool resources. Even in a repeated interaction game cooperation might not be enforceable and the groups sustain their costly appropriation efforts.

In general, political regimes in ethnically diverse countries are often found to be more engaged in inefficient "identity politics" than in more efficient "performance politics" (Collier, 1998). In the former situation, a political regime or party is supported not for its performance in terms of furthering prosperity, but for being led by people from the same group, while in the latter situation economic and political performance is rewarded. As most ethnically diverse countries are diverse at the national level and relatively homogeneous at the regional level, "identity politics" persist at the national level. With these politics people are reminded of differences and therefore an environment of low trust and cooperation is built and maintained. Collier (1998) argues that loyalty to ethnically-based parties is often maintained irrespective of economic performance and the government delivers patronage to the loyalists rather than services to the median voter.

A further disadvantage of high ethnic diversity is that it is believed to reduce the provision of public goods. Alesina, Baquir and Easterly (1999) formulate a model which links the heterogeneity of preferences across ethnic groups in a city to the amount and type of public goods the city supplies. A jurisdiction with two or more polarised groups (in the sense that these groups have preferences very far away from the median) would prefer to keep taxes low and deduct resources from the public good to private consumption. This results in a suboptimal provision of the public good which is then to the detriment of all.[1]

These theories may all lead to vicious cycles of high ethnic diversity,

[1] It should be noted that other forms of social distance, such as high income inequality or a geographical segregation of groups that could be unrelated to ethnic diversity, could also deliver such a result.

poor economic performance, and greater ethnic identification as a result since marginalised groups will build up even stronger identities in the face of poor economic performance and their social exclusion (Akerlof and Kranton, 2000).

In line with this argumentation, a society with a strong ethnic divide combined with a polarization of interests could be characterised by less altruism or/and a more pessimistic view of the future and thereby by lower savings. Walz (2001) argues that this phenomenon could be generated by strong immigration flows. Natives do not care about migrants as they do about fellow citizens and ethnic group members.

On the positive side, Lazear (1999) was one of the firsts to show that diversity can increase productivity. This effect arises because workers with different cultural backgrounds and skills are complementary. There is, however, a trade-off between the productive benefits of diversity and costs that occur due to possible difficulties in communication. Alesina and La Ferrara (2004) highlighted that the benefits of skill differentiation are more likely to be higher in more advanced and complex societies. Furthermore, ethnic or linguistic diversity which is due to immigration may improve trade opportunities for a country. Immigrants form ethnic networks between their home and host country (Casella and Rauch, 1997). Girma and Yu (2000) provide evidence that the trade-immigration linkage is driven by the new information brought by immigrants about their home country and not so much by existing business connections and personal contacts with their home country. This would mean that ethnic networks enhance trade between dissimilar countries. Gould (1994) describes the positive effect of co-ethnic networks as immigrants having links to their home country, which is like a human-capital externality that enhances trade opportunities (most likely between developed and developing countries). Trade is enhanced by a decrease in transaction costs to trade. Furthermore, bilateral trade flows are positively affected by the preference of immigrants for home country products. Gould (1994) finds that the trade enhancing effect is the strongest in the export sector and only a relatively small community of immigrants is needed to exhaust this effect. A relatively large community, however, is needed to exhaust the positive trade effect in the import sector. The hypothesis of the growth-enhancing effect of trade goes back to Adam Smith's (1776) argument of the division of labor. More recently endogenous growth theory led to learning-by-doing models which suggest that openness causes advanced economies to specialize in more advanced products where more learning-by-doing takes place and stimulates growth (Young, 1991).

Under world-wide free-trade regime countries may, however, enjoy the benefits of homogeneity and the diversity of production through international trade. Therefore Alesina, Spolaore and Wacziarg (2000) argued that countries would prefer to be more homogenous in this case.

Similarly, ethnic diversity of a country increases the attractiveness of that country to immigrants who often migrate to countries with existing networks of immigrants of the same origin. This increases the efficiency and adaptability of the labor market to economic change, and to the extent that the skills of the immigrants complement the home country population, is likely to improve the growth performance of that country. Lastly, ethnic diversity might be seen as beneficial because it increases the variety of products on offer in a country. As much of trade between rich countries is driven by such a taste for variety, there would logically be considerable benefit if such variety could be provided within one's own borders.

This paper aims to investigate the respective merits of the two theories on ethnic diversity and co-ethnic networks in an empirical analysis to complete the picture. We will investigate whether ethnic diversity has a growth enhancing effect in "immigration countries" which works against the negative effect of high ethnic diversity due to battles over scarce resources.

1.3 Existing Empirical Investigations

The pioneering paper by Easterly and Levine (1997), as well as a follow-up study by Alesina et al. (2003) argue that ethnic conflicts in the political sphere reduce economic growth by leading governments to adopt inefficient economic policies and low public good provision. Using cross-country seemingly unrelated regressions the authors show that the negative impact of ethnic fractionalisation operates via certain policy variables on growth. This link between ethnic diversity and the individual policy variable is further analysed by separate regressions which link ethnic fractionalisation significantly to the quality of policy and institutions. These identified channels have hurt Sub-Saharan Africa particularly, which had the highest measured fractionalisation and in turn had the lowest economic growth in the period of 1960-1990. For instance, the negative coefficient of the ethnic variable of -0.019[2] implies that Uganda has 1.77 percentage points lower annual growth in per capita income in the base line specification than South Korea which is merely due to different degrees of ethnic fractionalisation - 0.002 in South Korea versus 0.93 in Uganda.

As noted in the last section, other forms of social distance, especially income inequality could also lead to polarisation of interests between groups and therefore have identical implications for the economic perfor-

[2] See table 1.2

mance in a country. Easterly (2001) shows indeed that societies with a low class and income divide grow the fastest and the channels through which high ethnic diversity and high inequality have an impact on growth happen to be the same.

Moreover, extensions by Easterly (2001) show that the negative impact of high ethnic fractionalisation can be mitigated by strong institutions which they measure using the data from the International Country Risk Guide. These indicators measure the strength of the rule of law, judicial independence, bureaucratic quality, and protection of property rights. In countries with such strong institutions, the negative effect of ethnic fractionalisation on economic growth can be largely avoided (Easterly 2001).

Ottaviano and Peri (2004), as well as Sparber (2007), find evidence that ethnic diversity boosts productivity. Using a panel model Ottaviano and Peri (2004) show that linguistic diversity increases wages of white U.S. born males that are 40 to 50 years old.

No empirical study has considered the relationship between migration and ethnic fractionalisation and growth across countries so far. Several empirical studies find that immigrant links play an important role in determining bilateral trade flows. Gould (1994) shows that immigrants' ties to their home country play a key role in explaining bilateral trade flows of the U.S.. Girma and Yu(2000) investigate the link between immigration and trade using U.K. data. They find evidence that immigration from non-Commonwealth countries has a significant trade enhancing effect. Both studies find a pro-import, but most importantly pro-export effect. Several empirical studies give evidence on the growth-promoting effect of trade (volumes)(Levine and Renelt, 1992; Frankel and Romer, 1999; Acemoglu, 2005) and openness (Ades and Glaeser, 1999). However, a study of Rodríguez and Rodrik (2000) puts into question the hypothesis that *trade policies* trying to cut back trade barriers generate growth. When looking at the empirical literature on the relationship between foreign direct investment and growth, there seems to be a consensus that inbound foreign direct investment are advantageous for the economy, while not the same can be said on the effects of outbound foreign direct investment. Inbound foreign direct investments are found to be complementary to domestic investment (Feldstein, 1994; Desai et al., 2005).

Using a gravity model, Tong (2005) finds that Chinese networks, measured as the number of Chinese people in the country, are important correlate of bilateral foreign direct investment. She further investigates the mechanisms through which this co-ethnic network has an effect on cross-border investment. She finds that community enforcement of sanctions is important in countries with low bureaucratic quality. Furthermore, Chinese networks provide assistance in overcoming informational barriers.

1.4 Data and Methodology

Since our first objective was to update and extend the analysis of Alesina et al. we used the same variables and extended the dataset where possible using the same data sources to include the 1990s. This was possible for all variables except telephones per 1000 workers instead of which we introduced the variable telephones per 1000 people.[3] We decided to put the focus of our research on the ethnic fractionalisation variable "ethnic" only, which was constructed by Alesina et al. (2003). This is mainly due to the fact that we deemed it to be the most reasonable measure of

[3] Source: WDI 2003, this variable displays a very high correlation with the original variable telephone per 1000 workers. See appendix A table A.10

ethnic fractionalisation available to date.

The variable "ethnic" is measured by a one minus a Herfindahl concentration index

$$Fract_j = 1 - \sum_{i=1}^{N} {s_{ij}}^2 \tag{1.1}$$

where s_{ij} is the share of group i (i = 1,...,N) in country j. The index takes values from zero to one for each country. In practical terms, this index measures the probability that two randomly drawn individuals belong to a different ethnic group. The data to construct this index, i.e. the values for the group shares, are mainly taken from the Encyclopaedia Britannica (2001). A separate ethnic group is defined if there exist distinguishing linguistic and/or ethnic characteristics.

Table 1.1 shows the regional average of the different fractionalisation measures. Note that Sub-Saharan Africa displays the highest average index for all measures of fractionalisation. The index "ethnic" gives a more realistic picture of fractionalisation in Latin America than the ethnolinguistic measure (ELF) since this region is not primarily fractionalised linguistically but mostly due to ethnic groups.

Table 1.1: Sample Means of Fractionalisation Indices by Region

	ELF	Ethnic	Language	Religion
Latin America & Carribean	0.265	0.405	0.179	0.442
Sub-Saharan Africa	0.651	0.658	0.652	0.496
Eastern & Central Europe	0.315	0.366	0.32	0.491
Western & Southern Europe	0.147	0.177	0.196	0.311
Middle East	0.244	0.453	0.33	0.346
East & South East Asia	0.306	0.353	0.457	0.462

Source: Alesina et al. (2003). Note: ELF is Ethno-Linguistic Fractionalisation, constructed by Easterly and Levine (1997) using the Russian Atlas Narodov Mira

Thus, our dataset is structured as a four wave panel, which includes the time-invariant ethnic fractionalisation variable and past immigration dummy. In our empirical analysis we use the common methodology of Seemingly Unrelated Regressions (SUR). The model takes the following form:

$$growth_{1960} = \alpha_{1960} + \beta\mathbf{X}_{1960} + \gamma\mathbf{Z} + u_{1960} \quad (1.2)$$

$$growth_{1970} = \alpha_{1960} + \beta\mathbf{X}_{1970} + \gamma\mathbf{Z} + u_{1970} \quad (1.3)$$

$$growth_{1980} = \alpha_{1980} + \beta\mathbf{X}_{1980} + \gamma\mathbf{Z} + u_{1980} \quad (1.4)$$

$$growth_{1990} = \alpha_{1990} + \beta\mathbf{X}_{1990} + \gamma\mathbf{Z} + u_{1990} \quad (1.5)$$

Hence, growth is a function of a decade specific intercept alpha, a vector of variables X which vary across time t and countries i, a vector of variables Z which vary only across countries plus an error term.

Seemingly Unrelated Regressions is used for several particular reasons. First of all, it allowed us to be comparable with existing findings such as Easterly and Levine (1997) and Alesina et al. (2003). Secondly, and more importantly, pooled OLS is a valid estimation technique if there is no unobserved component c_i, that is if the error term is not serially correlated. A serially correlated error term can be described as follows:

$$v_{it} = c_i + u_{it} \tag{1.6}$$

If $\sigma_c^2 \neq 0$, then the error term is serially corelated and pooled OLS is inappropriate. Testing the presence of an unobserved effects is possible using a Breusch and Pagan statistic or a test statistic developed by Wooldridge that can reject the $H_0 = \sigma_c^2 = 0$ of serial correlation of errors even if the estimate for the variance of the unobserved effect σ_c^2 is negative. In our case the Breusch and Pagan statistic indicates that σ_c^2 is significantly different from zero and positive ($\sigma_c^2 > 0$).[4] The next step is to assess whether we can reliably estimate the partial effects using random effects estimation technique for panel data which is only possible if the explanatory variables are strictly exogenous to the unobserved effect. The conditional mean independence assumption demands that: $E(c_i \mid x_{i1}, ..., x_{iT}) = E(c_i)$. In our model we can compare the coefficients of the fixed and random effects method using the Hausman test. The test statistic[5] indicates that the difference between coefficients is systematic. Therefore random effects seems not to be the appropriate estimation technique.

Controlling for fixed effects and calculating within-estimators seems not to be advantageous for our research question. We can control for unobserved effects with the fixed effects method. But we cannot determine the effect of ethnic fractionalisation on growth, as this variable is time-invariant. However, it seems clearly problematic to assume that the influ-

4 $chi2(1) = 17.36, Prob > chi2 = 0.0000$

5 $chi2(6) = (b - B)'[(V_b - V_B)^{(-1)}](b - B) = 15.93$
$Prob > chi2 = 0.0141$

ence of the ethnicity variable on long-term growth does not incorporate geographical differences between Latin-America and Sub-Saharan Africa and the Western World but exclusively ethnic differences and their effect on growth. Furthermore, SUR allows the errors of the different equations to be correlated. In our setting, the cross-section unit is defined as the decade and therefore errors are allowed to be correlated across time. In other words, the effects of the independent variables on growth are allowed to be correlated within a country specific framework over time. Thus SUR should also yield efficient estimators.[6]

Furthermore, SUR seems clearly more favourable since it allows for a more detailed picture than a fixed effects estimation where effects are averaged over a 30 or 40 year horizon. With fixed effects we cannot allow for time-varying coefficients. SUR instead assigns a regression to each of the four decades, analysing the impact of a specific variable measured at the start of each decade on growth whereby this impact may be specified to differ between the decades or not. Therefore misspecification of the model can be controlled for as the heterogeneity of intercepts and coefficients is allowed. Moreover, SUR allows for a time invariant correlation between the independent variable and growth, but the estimates are derived by incorporating decade specific correlations.

The second aim of this paper was to combine the two existing strands of literature concerning the possibly counteracting impact of ethnic diversity on economic performance. Thus, we needed to define what constitutes an immigration country in order to single out the alleged positive impact of ethnic diversity due to immigration. There are many possible definitions of the variable "immigration country". However, we are in-

[6] The estimators would be biased if the residuals are correlated with the regressor or the residuals are correlated with the intercept. Even if the estimators are biased, they are more efficient.

terested in countries which are ethnically heterogeneous according to our measure and this to a large part due to past or more recent immigration. A country like Argentina, for example, has a population consisting up to 97 percent of Spanish and Italian descendants. Our definition therefore classifies a country as an immigration country if it was characterized by immigration from a non-neighboring country, forced or free, within the past 300 years and the descendants of foreign settlers constitute a significant part (at least 5 percent) of the population today. Most of these countries still have important migration networks with the former sending countries which explain why immigration into these countries is still high. We chose to include immigration from non-neighbouring countries only because we are interested in the effects of cultural diversity. Moreover, this variable is unsuspicious in regard to endogeneity. Data is taken from the CIA World Factbook, where the group share of ethnic groups and their origins are listed. Table A.9 in the appendix A lists the countries included in this definition.[7]

To get a first idea, the methodology we used to test for different effects of ethnic diversity in immigration and non-immigration countries is a simple interaction term between the immigration Dummy and the variable "ethnic". The hypothesis being that, if a country is classified as an immigration country, we would expect a distinct positive or at least compensating impact of ethnic diversity on growth. We analyze the underlying mechanism of the distinct positive effect of the interaction term using Seemingly Unrelated Regression also.

7 However, we cannot prove whether co-ethnic networks exist in each of these countries.

1.5 Results

1.5.1 Extending the Data Set

Before we start to analyse whether ethnic diversity has a distinct effect on growth in immigration countries, we want to confirm and update the baseline analysis by including the 1990s. The countries included in our analysis and the specific country-year combinations available can be found in the first four tables of appendix A. The results are noteworthy by themselves as they lend support to the original argument, namely, that high ethnic fractionalisation leads to an adverse policy environment, but also show some differences. Table 1.2 shows the results of the updated data analysis. The first two columns in table 1.2 reproduce the original findings of Alesina et al. with the difference that the variable "log telephones per worker" has been replaced by "log telephones per people" in regression (2).[8]

[8] To see the changes due to inclusion of this different variable in comparison with the original Alesina et al. results see appendix A table A.10

Table 1.2: Baseline Regression.

	Dependent Variable: Growth rate 1960-1980,1960-1999					
			Inclusion of 1990s			
Variable	(1)	(2)	(3)	(4)	(5)	(6)
Dummy Sub-Saharan Africa	-0.007	-0.013***	-0.010***	-0.011***	-0.014**	-0.014***
	(-1.53)	(-2.75)	(-2.50)	(-2.76)	(-3.22)	(-3.10)
Dummy Latin America/Caribbean	-0.018***	-0.017***	-0.015***	-0.013***	-0.011***	-0.014***
	(-4.85)	(-4.46)	(-4.61)	(-3.98)	(-3.29)	(-3.89)
Log of initial income	0.038*	0.067***	0.026	0.028*	0.04**	0.031
	(1.73)	(2.76)	(1.60)	(1.69)	(2.19)	(1.61)
Log of initial income squared	-0.003*	-0.006***	-0.002*	-0.002**	-0.003***	-0.003***
	(-1.93)	(-3.66)	(-1.94)	(-2.06)	(-2.77)	(-2.70)
Log of schooling	0.013***	0.005	0.012***	0.011***	0.011***	0.003
	(3.11)	(0.96)	(3.10)	(3.04)	(2.80)	(0.63)
Assassinations		-17.986*		-31.025***	-23.228***	-17.254**
		(-1.95)		(-3.16)	(-2.56)	(-2.42)
Financial Depth		0.011**			0.016***	0.012**
		(1.99)			(3.34)	(2.30)
Black Market Premium		-0.015***			-0.018***	-0.016***
		(-3.46)			(-4.81)	(-4.04)
Fiscal surplus/GDP		0.113***			0.102***	0.111***
		(3.64)			(3.64)	(3.89)
Log of telephones per people		0.022***				0.019***
		(3.64)				(3.31)
Ethnic	**-0.019*****	**-0.0040**	**-0.018*****	**-0.019*****	**-0.013****	**-0.009**
	(-2.96)	**(-0.55)**	**(-3.22)**	**(-3.22)**	**(-2.17)**	**(-1.50)**
Total Pool No. Obs.	264	179	356	349	267	257
Adj R2	0.38	0.57	0.34	0.35	0.47	0.5

Source: Own Calculations. Decade dummies not reported hear. Note: t-stats in parentheses *0.1, **0.05, ***0.01 Significance level. The regressions above were also estimated constraining the number of observations to 257 as in specification (4). Results are shown in tableA.11 in appendixA. Results provided on request. The countries included and the available year-country combinations are listed in the first four tables in appendixA.

The adverse impact of ethnic fractionalisation on growth via the policy environment is shown when comparing regressions (1) and (2) of table 1.2, as the inclusion of variables measuring the quality of the policy environment and public good provision renders the negative impact of "ethnic" to insignificance and strongly reduces the size of the coefficient.

If we now include data up to 1999, the following results can be observed. First of all, if we concentrate on specification (6), it confirms and strengthens the original findings that ethnic fractionalisation has a negative impact on growth as the results remain almost unchanged in terms of magnitude and significance. However, the coefficient of the Dummy for Sub-Saharan Africa gains in magnitude and significance. This hints at the continuing diverging growth experience of this region and the problem observed first by Easterly and Levine (1997) that the model cannot fully explain this diverging growth trend, even though high ethnic diversity is one of the main characteristics of this region.

Secondly, the variable "schooling" becomes again insignificant. The significance and magnitude of the other coefficients show not much variation. It is interesting that schooling becomes insignificant once we include telephone per thousand people. One possible explanation is that physical and human capital infrastructure is highly correlated for all decades. We find that the correlation coefficient between the level of schooling and telephones per thousand people takes a value of 0.83 in the 1960s, for the 1990s it has increased to 0.89.[9]

However, the most important finding is, once we include data for

[9] Pritchett (1999) analyses why education has no significant influence on growth in a cross-country setting and suggests three different explanations. First of all, it might be the case that indeed schooling creates no human capital. Secondly, the marginal returns to human capital are falling rapidly where demand for educated labour is stagnant. Lastly, the institutional environments in many countries have been sufficiently perverse that the human capital accumulated has been applied to activities that served to reduce economic growth.

the 1990s, that we find a remaining effect of ethnic fractionalisation on growth, even after the inclusion of the policy variables. In the 1990s, the effect of ethnic fractionalisation remains significant at the 1 percent level, if we do not restrict the coefficient to be the same across decades. This can be seen in table 1.3.[10] The effect of ethnic fractionalisation on growth in the 1990s is not mitigated by the inclusion of the policy variables.

Table 1.3: 1990s Effect.

	Growth rate 1960-1999
Variable	
Dummy for the 1960s	-0.077
	(-0.97)
Dummy for the 1970s	-0.070
	(-0.89)
Dummy for the 1980s	-0.088
	(-1.12)
Dummy for the 1990s	-0.079
	(-1.01)
Dummy for Sub-Saharan Africa	-0.014***
	(-3.20)
Dummy for Latin America & Caribbean	-0.014***
	(-4.24)
Log of initial income	0.041**
	(2.14)
Log of initial income squared	-0.004***
	(-3.30)
Log of schooling	0.004
	(0.83)
Assassinations	-2.204***
	(-2.51)
Financial Depth	0.012***
	(2.48)

[10] The countries included and the available year-country combinations are listed in the first four tables in appendix A. Residuals are displayed in figure A.1 and A.2 in appendix A. No particular pattern is found in the residual distribution that would hint at violation of the most important assumptions of OLS (zero expected value, constant variance, statistical independence).

Black Market Premium	-0.016*** (-4.23)
Fiscal surplus/GDP	0.117*** (4.21)
Log of telephones per people	0.020*** (3.69)
Ethnic 1960	0.001 (0.12)
Ethnic 1970	-0.007 (-0.78)
Ethnic 1980	-0.005 (-0.60)
Ethnic 1990	**-0.023*** (-2.55)**
No. Obs.	38;67;74;78
Adj R2	0.11;0.36;0.47;0.18

Source: Own Calculations. Note: t-stats in parentheses *0.1, **0.05, ***0.01 Significance level. The countries included and the available year-country combinations are listed in the first four tables in appendix A. Residuals are displayed in figure A.1 and A.2 in appendix A. No particular pattern is found in the residual distribution that would hint at violation of the most important assumptions of OLS (zero expected value, constant variance, statistical independence).

This must be due to the fact that ethnic diversity has gained a bigger impact on growth in the 1990s. To further validate the finding, we ran a separate regression for each decade to assess whether the impact of "ethnic" increased between the 1960s and the 1990s. The results indicate that this is indeed the case as the only decade in which "ethnic" has a negative significant impact, even after the inclusion of the policy variables, are the 1990s. For all other decades the impact of "ethnic" in the extended regression is not statistically different from zero. The findings are shown in table 1.4.

Table 1.4: Decade Specific Growth Regression.

	Growth rate for noted decades							
Variable	1960		1970		1980		1990	
	(1)	(2)	(3)	(4)	(5)	(6)	(7)	(8)
Dummy for the 1960s	-0.3644*	-0.2611						
	(-1.72)	(-0.93)						
Dummy for the 1970s			-0.4914**	-0.4296**				
			(-2.76)	(-1.98)				
Dummy for the 1980s					-0.2014	-0.1880		
					(-1.61)	(-1.44)		
Dummy for the 1990s							-0.0376	0.0652
							(-0.23)	(0.37)
Dummy for Sub-Saharan Africa	-0.0148	-0.0198*	-0.0092	-0.0066	-0.0105	-0.0123	-0.0176***	-0.0165***
	(-1.35)	(-1.68)	(-1.22)	(-0.88)	(-1.62)	(-1.77)	(-2.36)	(-2.10)
Dummy for Latin America& Caribbean	-0.0206***	-0.0245***	-0.0154***	-0.0155***	-0.0296***	-0.0210***	-0.0099*	-0.0073
	(-3.10)	(-3.04)	(-2.49)	(-2.28)	(-5.59)	(-3.63)	(-1.79)	(-1.06)
Log of initial income	0.1064*	0.0899	0.1431***	0.1454***	0.0549*	0.0643	0.0171	0.0040
	(1.91)	(1.25)	(3.10)	(2.70)	(1.72)	(1.95)	(0.43)	(0.10)
Log of initial income squared	-0.0074*	-0.0070	-0.0098**	-0.0119***	-0.0036*	-0.0053***	-0.0013	-0.0013
	(-2.01)	(-1.50)	(-3.25)	(-3.40)	(-1.74)	(-2.43)	(-0.57)	(-0.56)
Log of schooling	0.0174**	0.0127	0.0152**	0.0058	0.0118*	0.0040	0.0086	0.0015
	(1.96)	(1.25)	(2.10)	(0.76)	(1.74)	(0.47)	(1.09)	(0.14)
Assassinations		51.937		-17.867		-14.798		-86.466**
		(0.87)		(-1.06)		(-1.33)		(-2.06)
Financial Depth		-0.0003		0.0054		0.0145		0.0097
		(-0.03)		(0.48)		(1.63)		(1.06)
Black Market Premium		-0.0180		-0.0286***		-0.0085		-0.0211**
		(-1.07)		(-2.75)		(-1.54)		(-2.19)
Fiscal surplus/GDP		0.0724		0.1988***		0.1339***		0.1758***
		(0.56)		(2.82)		(3.33)		(2.49)
Log of telephones per people		0.0117		0.0395***		0.0212**		0.0150
		(0.84)		(3.89)		(2.05)		(1.11)
Ethnic	**-0.0069**	**0.0008**	**-0.0256*****	**0.0048**	**-0.0153***	**-0.0008**	**-0.0120*****	**-0.0193***
	(-0.54)	**(0.06)**	**(-2.35)**	**(0.41)**	**(-1.66)**	**(-0.08)**	**(-2.44)**	**(-1.83)**
No. Obs.	38	38	88	67	94	74	92	78
Adj R2	0.23	0.37	0.28	0.62	0.38	0.59	0.15	0.29

Source: Own Calculations. Note: t-stats in parentheses *0.1, **0.05, ***0.01 Significance level.

Moreover, we ran a completely unrestricted version of our SUR model, which means that we loosened the restriction that coefficients have to be the same across decades for all variables except the decade dummies. The results are shown in table A.6 in appendix A. The regression clearly shows that policy variables have very distinct effects in different decades, that conditional β-convergence can only be found in two decades, and that ethnic fractionalisation has a sizeable impact on growth in the 1990s besides the policy variables. Therefore, we may well conclude that the model proposed by Alesina et al. (2003) is incomplete and may not be stable across decades.

We tested several other models to explain the negative impact of ethnic fractionalisation on growth in the 1990s. Good governance seems to mitigate the influence of fractionalisation on growth. When including the Kaufman-Kraay-Zoido-Lobaton-Indicator in our regression the variable "ethnic" becomes insignificant (see table 1.5).[11]

Table 1.5: Unrestricted SUR Model including Kaufmann, Kraay and Zoido-Lobaton Index.

	Growth rate 1960-1999	
Variable	Coefficient	t-Statistic
Dummy for the 1960s	-0.325	(-1.44)
Dummy for the 1970s	-0.437**	(-2.45)
Dummy for the 1980s	-0.277**	(-2.37)
Dummy for the 1990s	0.135	(-0.71)
1960s		
Africa	-0.018***	(-1.88)
Latin America	-0.015**	(-2.17)
Log of initial income	0.116**	(2.01)

11 Many observations are lost when including the governance index. We therefore ran the model without the governance variable for the same numbers of observation. Ethnic fractionalisation remains significant in explaining growth. The results are shown in table A.7 in appendix A

Log of initial income squared	-0.010*	(-2.59)
Log of schooling	0.011	(1.40)
Assassinations	56.408	(1.27)
Financial Depth	0.026**	(2.13)
Black Market Premium	-0.016	(-0.92)
Fiscal surplus/GDP	0.009	(0.08)
Log of telephones per people	0.021***	(1.81)
Ethnic	**0.006**	**(0.58)**
Kaufmann, Kraay and Z.-L.-I.	0.007	(1.34)
Adj R2	0.38	
Observations	36	
1970s		
Africa	-0.011	(-1.44)
Latin America	-0.016*	(-2.81)
Log of initial income	0.143*	(3.14)
Log of initial income squared	-0.011*	(-3.73)
Log of schooling	0.004	(0.61)
Assassinations	-18.421	(-1.46)
Financial Depth	0.003	(0.31)
Black Market Premium	-0.035*	(-3.95)
Fiscal surplus/GDP	0.174*	(3.04)
Log of telephones per people	0.031*	(3.67)
Ethnic	**0.009**	**(0.84)**
Kaufmann, Kraay and Z.-L.-I.	-0.002	(-0.30)
Adj R2	0.52	
Observations	57	
1980s		
Africa	-0.019*	(-2.92)
Latin America	-0.028*	(-5.30)
Log of initial income	0.088*	(2.94)
Log of initial income squared	-0.006*	(-3.32)
Log of schooling	-0.004	(-0.51)
Assassinations	-19.084**	(-2.32)
Financial Depth	0.007	(1.01)
Black Market Premium	-0.008***	(-1.68)
Fiscal surplus/GDP	0.099*	(2.90)
Log of telephones per people	0.017**	(2.02)
Ethnic	**-0.008**	**(-0.84**
Kaufmann, Kraay and Z.-L.-I.	0.004	(0.77)
Adj R2	0.56	
Observations	63	
1990s		

Africa	-0.017**	(-1.99)
Latin America	-0.010	(-1.34)
Log of initial income	0.054	(1.18)
Log of initial income squared	-0.004***	(-1.68)
Log of schooling	0.013	(1.24)
Assassinations	-52.058	(-1.42)
Financial Depth	0.002	(0.28)
Black Market Premium	-0.018	(-1.34)
Fiscal surplus/GDP	0.120***	(1.68)
Log of telephones per people	0.004	(0.30)
Ethnic	**-0.016**	**(-1.40)**
Kaufmann, Kraay and Z.-L.-I.	0.011***	(1.73)
Adj R2	0.22	
Observations	65	
No. Obs.	257	

Source: Own Calculations. *0.1, **0.05, ***0.01 Significance level. Residuals are displayed in figure A.3 and A.4 in appendixA. No particular pattern is found in the residual distribution that would hint at violation of the most important assumptions of OLS (zero expected value, constant variance, statistical independence).

Ethnic fractionalisation may lead to inefficient "identity" politics instead of efficient "performance" politics (Collier, 1998). The index measures governance in the dimensions graft, rule of law, voice and accountability, political instability and violence, government effectiveness, and regulatory burden. Governance seems to have gained importance for growth in the 1990s. This may partly be explained by the withdrawal of influence by the two superpowers from many regions of the world with the end of the Cold War. Proving this hypothesis through regressing ethnic fractionalisation on the governance index, confirms the hypothesis. High fractionalisation has a significant negative effect on good governance in each decade as can be seen in table 1.6 below.[12]

[12] Residuals are displayed in figure A.5 and A.6 in appendix A. No particular pattern is found in the residual distribution.

Table 1.6: Indirect Effect of Fractionalisation on Good Governance.

	Dependent Variable: KKZ- Index	
Variable	Coefficient	t-Statistic
Dummy for the 1960s	-1,153***	(-3,60)
Dummy for the 1970s	-1,292***	(-3,95)
Dummy for the 1980s	-1,467***	(-4,44)
Dummy for the 1990s	-1,673***	(-4,89)
Africa	0,147	(1,18)
Latin America	-0,323***	(-3,34)
Log of initial income	0,242***	(6,70)
Log of schooling	0,279***	(4,19)
Dependency Ratio	-0,309*	(-1,92)
	1960s	
Ethnic	**-1,071*****	**(-5,58)**
Adj R2	0,63	
Observations	69	
	1970s	
Ethnic	**-1,028*****	**(-5,65)**
Adj R2	0,67	
Observations	71	
	1980s	
Ethnic	**-0,929*****	**(-5,07)**
Adj R2	0,66	
Observations	72	
	1990s	
Ethnic	**-0,802*****	**(-4,06)**
Adj R2	0,63	
Observations	74	
No. Obs.	286	

Source: Own Calculations. *0.1, **0.05, ***0.01 Significance level. Note that the schooling variable and the dependency ratio could be excluded from the regression without a signficant change in the results. Residuals are displayed in figure A.5 and A.6in appendix A. No particular pattern is found in the residual distribution.

Furthermore, if the impact of ethnic fractionalisation is differing in the four decades, it might also differ between regions. The sample is therefore divided into two subgroups. As we do not have sufficient numbers of observations to analyse the model for Sub-Saharan Africa and Latin America separately, we combined both to one group including 73 countries. We compare this with "the rest of the world" including 63 OECD, Asian and some Arabic countries. The results are shown in table 1.7. Strikingly, the results differ very much between the two subgroups. Considering Sub-Saharan Africa and Latin America, the impact of the variable measuring ethnic fractionalisation, however, remains significant only at the 10 percent level after the inclusion of the policy variables.

Contrarily, in the "rest of the world" the hypothesis of Alesina et al. and Easterly and Levine seems to explain the growth differences between countries rather well. Inefficient policies and low public good provision explain the diverging growth trends, which are partly due to ethnic fractionalisation. In these regions it seems to be indeed the case that the transmission channel of high ethnic fractionalisation and its negative impact on growth can be explained by an adverse policy environment alone. Thus, the obtained results show that the negative impact of ethnic fractionalisation on growth above and beyond the policy control variables prevails only in the 1990s and in the regions of Sub-Saharan Africa and Latin America.

The above approach, however, faces the problem that few observations remain when restricting the sample to Sub-Saharan and Latin-American countries. In order to verify the findings we included an interaction term for ethnic fractionalisation in Sub-Saharan Africa. The results clearly show that the remaining negative impact of ethnic fractionalisation on economic growth is captured in the last interaction term for ethnic fractionalisation in Sub-Saharan Africa in the regression pre-

Table 1.7: Sub-Saharan African and Latin American Results.

	Dependent Variable: Growth rate 1960-1999			
Variable	Africa and Latinam		Rest of the World	
	(1)	(2)	(3)	(4)
Dummy for the 1960s	0.127	-0.037	-0.249***	0.006
	(1.2)	(-0.30)	(-2.58)	(0.05)
Dummy for the 1970s	0.125	-0.033	-0.249***	0.008
	(1.17)	(-0.27)	(-2.58)	(0.06)
Dummy for the 1980s	0.099	-0.053	-0.262***	-0.005
	(0.93)	(-0.43)	(-2.72)	(-0.04)
Dummy for the 1990s	0.12	-0.054	-0.256***	0.004
	(1.03)	(-0.44)	(-2.68)	(0.03)
Log of initial income	-0.026	0.03	0.076***	0.026
	(-0.93)	(0.94)	(3.21)	(0.86)
Log of initial income squared	0.002	-0.003	-0.005***	-0.004**
	(0.81)	(-1.50)	(-3.63)	(-2.06)
Log of schooling	0.011**	-0.004	0.011**	0.008
	(1.98)	(0.54)	(2.25)	(1.54)
Assassinations		-24.819***		-16.353
		(-2.57)		(-0.76)
Financial Depth		0.036***		0.01*
		(2.33)		(1.84)
Black Market Premium		-0.015***		-0.018***
		(-2.82)		(-2.87)
Fiscal surplus/GDP		0.113***		0.083*
		(2.84)		(1.95)
Log of telephones per people		0.022***		0.026***
		(2.48)		(3.26)
Ethnic	**-0.014***	**-0.016***	**-0.019*****	**-0.001**
	(-1.81)	**(-1.77)**	**(-2.52)**	**(-0.063)**
Total Pool No. Obs.	181	105	175	114
Adj R2	0.23	0.42	0.24	0.39

Source: Own Calculations. Note: t-stats in parentheses *0.1, **0.05, ***0.01 Significance level.

sented in table 1.8.[13] The variable "ethnic" which captures the residual effect of ethnic fractionalisation in general, is no longer statistically significant. The overall effect of the interaction term is on average -0.032[14], which implies that the inclusion of the policy variables did not change the negative impact of ethnic fractionalisation on growth for Sub-Saharan African countries. These results confirm the hypothesis that the remaining negative impact of ethnic fractionalisation on growth, even after the inclusion of policy variables, is in particular a Sub-Saharan phenomenon.

Table 1.8: SSA Effect.

	Growth rate 1960-1999
Variable	
Dummy for the 1960s	0.029
	(0.38)
Dummy for the 1970s	0.032
	(0.41)
Dummy for the 1980s	0.015
	(0.19)
Dummy for the 1990s	0.017
	(0.23)
Dummy for Sub-Saharan Africa	0.015
	(1.61)
Dummy for Latin America & Caribbean	-0.014***
	(-4.39)
Log of initial income	0.015
	(0.80)
Log of initial income squared	-0.002**
	(-2.04)

13 We also tested for a Latin American*Ethnic interaction term, however, there was no specific Latin American impact.

14 This is the coefficient of the interaction term multiplied by the average ethnic fractionalisation in SSA (-0.049*0.658). However, this effect should be interpreted jointly with the SSA effect, which is positive, but just below the 10 percent significance level (p-value = 0.1079). Then the overall effect becomes -0.017 of ethnic fragmentation in Sub-Saharan Africa. Also generally interesting to note that the SSA dummy is almost statistically significantly positive which would imply a stronger than average growth in SSA once the effect of ethnic fractionalisation is accounted for.

Log of schooling	0.003 (0.64)
Assassinations	-21.526** (-2.48)
Financial Depth	0.011** (2.31)
Black Market Premium	-0.016*** (-4.30)
Fiscal surplus/GDP	0.105*** (3.85)
Log of telephones per people	0,022*** (4.08)
Ethnic	**-0.001** **(-0.13)**
Ethnic x SSA	**-0.049***** **(-3.40)**
Total Pool No. Obs.	257
Adj R2	0.53

Source: Own Calculations. Note: t-stats in parentheses *0.1, **0.05, ***0.01 Significance level.

Given the above results, we wanted to test for the hypothesis that violent civil conflicts could explain this region specific effect of ethnic fractionalisation even though existing research found robust evidence that ethnic polarisation not fractionalisation explains civil conflict (Montalvo and Reynal-Querol, 2005).[15] This hypothesis is conceivable as conflict incidences increased substantially between the 1960s and the 1990s and are concentrated in particular in countries of Sub-Saharan Africa and Latin America, as confirmed by the Prio Database of the International Peace Research Institute Oslo.[16] However, our empirical results cannot support

[15] Even though civil conflict is better explained by ethnic polarisation than by ethnic fractionalisation those two concepts are sufficiently correlated to control empirically if the inclusion of a violent conflict variables renders the impact of the ethnic fractionalisation variable above and beyond the inclusion of the policy variables on growth to insignificance.

[16] Prio Database of the International Peace Research Institute Oslo, www.prio.no. The database reports the crude measure of numbers of conflicts as follows: 82

the hypothesis above because the correlation between ethnic fractionalisation and violent conlict is low and the influence of the violent conflict variables on growth is not significantly different from zero.[17] Thus, at least the variable specifications we used for violent civil conflicts cannot explain the remaining sizable negative effect of the ethnic fractionalisation variable on growth after the inclusion of policy variables in the 1990s or for Sub-Saharan Africa and Latin America.

If not violent conflict, what is the channel through which ethnic fractionalisation is having the effect on growth in Sub-Saharan Africa? Table 1.9 below shows that the effect of ethnic fractionalisation in Sub-Saharan Africa seems to be mitigated by the inclusion of governance, as well as investment in the restricted SUR model. In the unrestricted model (see appendix A, table A.8), investment renders the effect to insignificance[18]. Investment is included instead of the policy variables as they are highly correlated with investment. We find that ethnic fractionalisation in general is effective through governance. Specifically in Sub-Saharan Africa, we find a channel via investment on growth (see table 1.10 and 1.11 below). Moreover, this effect is only found in the 1990s.

---

incidences of violent conflict beginning in the 1960s (34 of which took place in Sub-Saharan Africa and Latin America), 87 in the1970s (33 of which took place in SSA and LA), 102 in the 1980s (30 of which took place in SSA and LA), jumping to 172 incidences at the beginning of the 1990s in the whole world (77 of which took place in SSA and LA). Even though this measure holds no information concerning the intensity and duration of violent conflict it confirms the sheer fact that the incidences of civil conflict has increased dramatically in the 1990s and that they were mostly concentrated in Sub-Saharan and Latin America.

17 The variable "ethnic" does not lose significance when including a variable for violent conflict in the regression. The results are not reported here. Data is from the Prio Database. Multiple definitions of violent civil conflicts were tested: minor-, intermediate civil conflict, civil war (internal and internationalised internal) and frequency in a decade. None of this specifications produced significant results.

18 With the exception of the second decade, the 1970s, this is indeed the case.

This is a new finding as the general effect of ethnic fractionalisation on growth seems to work via public goods provision, as measured by government transfers subsidies as percentage of GDP and infrastructure quality (Alesina et al., 2003). In Sub-Saharan Africa instead and in the 1990s especially investment seems to be impeded in a fractionalised society.

Table 1.9: SSA Effect including Investment and the Kaufmann, Kraay and Zoido-Lobaton- Index.

	Growth rate 1960-1999			
Variable				
Dummy for the 1960s	-0.055	-0.159**	-0.074	-0.160**
	(-0.83)	(-2.07)	(-1.03)	(-2.16)
Dummy for the 1970s	-0.057	-0.160**	-0.077	-0.160**
	(-0.86)	(-2.08)	(-1.08)	(-2.16)
Dummy for the 1980s	-0.077	-0.176***	-0.09	-0.175**
	(-1.16)	(-2.28)	(-1.32)	(-2.36)
Dummy for the 1990s	-0.070	-0.162**	-0.090	-0.160**
	(-1.05)	(-2.12)	(-1.21)	(-2.17)
Dummy Sub-Saharan Africa	0.007	0.002	0.011	0.0001
	(0.81)	(0.14)	(1.07)	(0.01)
Dummy Latin America/Caribbean	-0.015***	-0.017***	-0.015***	-0.015***
	(-4.72)	(-5.06)	(-4.68)	(-4.62)
Log of initial income	0.026	0.057***	0.030*	0.057***
	(1.53)	(2.93)	(1.68)	(3.05)
Log of initial income sq.	-0.002**	-0.004***	-0.002**	-0.004***
	(-1.84)	(-3.42)	(-2.02)	(-3.64)
Log of schooling	0.011***	0.002	0.008**	0.002
	(2.96)	(0.52)	(1.98)	(0.37)
Investment as perc. of GDP			0.0003**	0.0003*
			(2.28)	(1.90)
Kaufmann, Kraay and Z.-L.-Index		0.011***		0.012***
		(3.73)		(3.94)
Ethnic	**-0.012***	**0.004**	**-0.007**	**0.004**
	(-1.83)	**(0.55)**	**(-1.07)**	**(0.58)**
Ethnic x SSA	**-0.029****	**-0.040***	**-0.039*****	**-0.034**
	(-2.26)	**(-1.68)**	**(-2.57)**	**(-1.61)**
Total Pool No. Obs.	356	282	336	280
Adj R2	0.36	0.40	0.35	0.42

Source: Own Calculations. Note: t-stats in parentheses *0.1, **0.05, ***0.01 Significance level.

Table 1.10: Indirect Effect of Fragmentation in SSA.

	Investment 1960-1999	Governance
Dummy for the 1960s	-23.186	3.729*
	(-0.87)	(1.67)
Dummy for the 1970s	-22.637	3.558
	(-0.85)	(1.59)
Dummy for the 1980s	-25.877	3.408
	(-0.97)	(1.52)
Dummy for the 1990s	27.258	3.177
	(-1.02)	(1.42)
Dummy for Sub-Saharan Africa	1.90	0.025
	(0.46)	(0.05)
Dummy for Latin America & Caribbean	-4.116***	-0.332***
	(-2.68)	(-2.92)
Log of initial income	9.362	-1.314**
	(1.41)	(-2.35)
Log of initial income squared	-0.382	0.119***
	(-0.92)	(3.42)
Dependency Ratio	-8.312*	
	(-1.82)	
Ethnic	-0.311	-0.564**
	(-0.10)	(-2.43)
Ethnic x SSA	-7.331	-0.113
	(-1.23)	(-0.16)
Total Pool No. Obs.	415	316
Adj R2	0.42	0.73

Source: Own Calculations. Note: t-stats in parentheses *0.1, **0.05, ***0.01 Significance level.

Table 1.11: Indirect Effect of Fragmentation in SSA - Decade Specific.

	Investment 1960-1999
Variable	
Dummy for the 1960s	-1.789 (-0.09)
Dummy for the 1970s	-1.467 (-0.08)
Dummy for the 1980s	-5.040 (-0.27)
Dummy for the 1990s	-7.777 (-0.42)
Dummy for Latin America & Caribbean	-4.764 (-3.95)
Log of initial income	5.011 (1.06)
Log of schooling	-0.151 (-0.51)
Dependency Ratio	-8.951*** (-2.79)
1960s	

Dummy for Sub-Saharan Africa	-2.637 (-0.45)
Ethnic	-2.753 (-0.65)
Ethnic x SSA	-2.741 (-0.31)
Adj R2	0.27
Observations	100
1970s	
Dummy for Sub-Saharan Africa	1.276 (0.227)
Ethnic	-2.864 (-0.71)
Ethnic x SSA	-5.967 (-0.72)
Adj R2	0.26
Observations	102
1980s	
Dummy for Sub-Saharan Africa	0.693 (0.19)
Ethnic	-1.769 (-0.65)
Ethnic x SSA	-5.079 (-0.95)
Adj R2	0.55
Observations	102
1990s	
Dummy for Sub-Saharan Africa	10.998*** (2.96)
Ethnic	2.806 (0.94)
Ethnic x SSA	-22.592*** (-4.00)
Adj R2	0.50
Observations	111
Total System Obs.	415

Source: Own Calculations. Note: t-stats in parentheses *0.1, **0.05, ***0.01 Significance level. A similar regression was run for governance. In each decade there is no significant effect of ethnic fractionalizaion on governance. Residuals are displayed in figure A.7 and A.8 in appendixA. No particular pattern is found in the residual distribution that hints at the violation of the assumptions of OLS.

To sum up, we find a remaining direct negative effect of fractionalisation on growth in the 1990s and in Sub-Saharan Africa. The specific 1990s effect of fractionalisation can be explained by bad governance and the consequential growth hampering effect. If we look at Sub-Saharan Africa, the 1990s effect of fractionalisation on growth works via reduced investment. This means that a highly fractionalised society in Sub-Saharan Africa in which governments point at ethnic differences and instrumentalise ethnic differences to stay in power, create a poor investment climate.

1.5.2 Migration and Ethnic Fractionalisation

The second aim of this paper is to reconcile the two theoretical arguments of the different effects of fractionalisation and immigration on growth presented in the first part of this paper. So far we have argued empirically that fractionalisation of groups is problematic as it leads to conflicts of political nature, hampering growth. Now, we hypothesise that countries, in which ethnic fractionalisation partially emerged because of settlement and immigration, should also experience positive effects of diversity and not only negative effects. We do not argue that in immigration countries, which are fractionalised, models which explain inefficient policies and low public good provision are no longer valid. We rather investigate whether positive effects of immigration also prevail and which effect dominates in a cross-country setting. Before turning to our empirical analysis of this issue, we would like to highlight some of our constraints in testing the hypothesis. First of all, to draw a clear definition of what constitutes an "immigration country", is less straightforward for our purpose. As described above, our definition classifies a country as an immigration country if it was characterized by immigration from a non-neighboring country, forced or free, within the past 300 years and the descendants of foreign settlers or immigrants that were attracted through the persistance of migration networks constitute a significant part (at least 5 percent) of the population today. Thus there should be considerable ethnic diversity due to settlement and/or immigration in those countries. Furthermore, the cultural differences that are present between non-neighbouring, that is dissimilar countries, lead to potentially growth enhancing effects through trade enhancement, skill complementarities in the labour market, and/or the willingness of immigrants to invest in their host country due to the decision to stay long-term. Secondly, the theory of co-ethnic networks is only tested superficially in our setting. Usually, the theory on co-ethnic networks is tested by analysing the relationship between the inflow of migrants and trade using panel data. Ethnic fractionalisation, however, is assumed to be time-invariant and the networks we look at have been in existence for a long time.[19]

Utilising the updated dataset, we tested whether there is a distinguished effect of ethnic fractionalisation on economic performance in countries which are ethnically diverse partly due to foreign immigration. The argument being that those countries which display high ethnic diversity, partly due to immigration, might be capable to reap the benefits of such an increased diversity via increased trade, productivity, or investment gains.

Our results indicate that there is indeed a distinct effect of ethnic fractionalisation in immigration countries (see Table 1.12). Countries that can be characterized by foreign long-term immigration seem to exhibit positive effects of ethnic fractionalisation on subsequent growth.

The coefficient of the interaction-term implies that the negative effect of ethnic diversity on long-run growth is more than mitigated. There is

[19] Countries like the USA have experienced massive immigration flows over the past 40 years and therefore its ethnic composition might have changed significantly. Constructing a time-varying index would require sound data on ethnic compositions over the last 40 years. This is a potential future research topic.

positive mitigating effect in countries that are diverse due to immigration. If the policy variables which measure the quality of governmental policy are taken into account, the interaction-term stays significant at the 5 percent level. The average size of the effect of ethnic fractionalisation on growth is therefore reduced to -0.007 in immigration countries. Economic growth would decrease by 0.7 percentage points if the ethnic index would change from complete homogeneity to complete heterogeneity.[20]

Table 1.12: Past Settlement, Immigration, Ethnic Fractionalisation and Growth.

	Dependent Variable: Growth rate 1960-1999		
Variable	(1)	(2)	(3)
Dummy for the 1960s	-0.042	-0.042	0.015
	(0.60)	(0.59)	(0.18)
Dummy for the 1970s	-0.045	-0.044	0.019
	(0.63)	(0.61)	(0.22)
Dummy for the 1980s	-0.066	-0.065	0.001
	(-0.92)	(-0.90)	(0.01)
Dummy for the 1990s	-0.060	-0.059	0.002
	(0.83)	(0.81)	(0.02)
Dummy for Sub-Saharan Africa	0.000	-0.001	-0.004
	(0.04)	(0.29)	(0.76)
Log of initial income	0.036**	0.036**	0.027**
	(2.01)	(1.99)	(1.29)
Log of initial income squared	-0.003**	-0.003**	-0.003
	(2.44)	(2.43)	(2.31)
Dependency Ratio	-0.047***	-0.043***	-0.034***
	(3.93)	(3.58)	(2.63)
Log of schooling	0.007*	0.007	0.000
	(1.75)	(1.61)	(0.047)
Assassinations		-27.37**	-21.43**
		(2.48)	(2.13)
Financial Depth			0.016***
			(2.90)
Black Market Premium			-0.018***
			(4.29)
Fiscal surplus/GDP			0.119***

20 This is the effect of average ethnic fractionalisation in immigration countries 0,429 times 0.027 plus (-0.019).

			(3.81)
Log of telephones per people			0.015**
			(2.41)
Ethnic	-0.029***	-0.030***	-0.019**
	(3.64)	(3.79)	(2.18)
Immigration Dummy	-0.019***	-0.017***	-0.014**
	(3.39)	(3.11)	(2.36)
Immigration*Ethnic	0.034***	0.034)***	0.027**
	(2.71)	(2.76)	(2.03)
Total Pool No. Obs.	356	349	257
Adj R2	0.36	0.37	0.50

Source: Own Calculations. Note: t-stats in parentheses *0.1, **0.05, ***0.01 Significance level. Note also that the Latinam Dummy is left out because it is highly correlated with the Immigration Dummy.

The hypothesized channel of the co-ethnic trading network theory would ascribe the remaining positive effect on growth to trade. Ethnic networks created in the past may persist today and foster trade or foreign direct investment. We investigate further whether a growth enhancing effect of high ethnic fractionalisation via a trade channel prevails in immigration countries.[21] However, we cannot confirm this trade channel, as we find no evidence of a positive relationship between ethnic diversity and trade in our immigration countries. Ethnic diversity in immigration countries is not significant determinant of foreign direct investments or exports.[22]

These results leave the question of the channels through which ethnic

21 Trade is defined as exports and imports as a share of GDP, which increased dramatically between the 1960s and 1990s in most countries and also displayed an increased variation between countries. However, both patterns of change cannot be explained by our timeinvariant variable 'ethnic fractionalisation' which is assumed to be constant over the 40 year horizon. However, we would like to point out that a change in the ethnic index would require substantive migration flows and thus even if a time variant variable "ethnic" would be generated, we would expect it to be characterised by none or little and very slowly change over time and thus would be most likely no suitable variable to explain rapid change in trade patterns.

22 Results are not reported here, but available on request.

fractionalisation in immigration countries has an influence on long-run growth. According to Acemoglu (2001), in countries where settlers were not exposed to tropic diseases, settlers had a longer-term perspective and therefore replicated European institutions. These institutions lay ground for a favorable economic development after the end of colonization. The argument also implies that long-term migrants are willing to invest in the host-country.

Consistent with Acemoglu (2001), we find that ethnic diversity in immigration countries has a positive indirect effect through investment on growth. This can be seen in table 1.13 and table 1.14.

Table 1.13: Explanatory Channels of Past Settlement and Ethnic Fractionalisation

	Dependent Variable: Growth rate 1960-1999		
Variable	(1)	(2)	(3)
Dummy for the 1960s	-0.060	-0.021	-0.070
	(-0.75)	(-0.28)	(-0.90)
Dummy for the 1970s	-0.061	-0.024	-0.070
	(-0.76)	(-0.33)	(-0.91)
Dummy for the 1980s	-0.078	-0.044	-0.087
	(-0.98)	(-0.59)	(-1.13)
Dummy for the 1990s	-0.066	-0.036	-0.074
	(-0.84)	(-0.48)	(-0.96)
Dummy for Sub-Saharan Africa	-0.011	-0.004	-0.013
	(-2.18)	(-0.80)	(-2.50)
Log of initial income	0.046**	0.029	0.046**
	(2.35)	(1.59)	(2.47)
Log of initial income squared	-0.004***	-0.002**	-0.004***
	(-2.99)	(-2.08)	(-3.19)
Dependency Ratio	-0.052***	-0.043***	-0.046***
	(-4.16)	(-3.54)	(-3.68)
Log of schooling	-0.001	0.005	-0.001
	(-0.131)	(1.19)	(-0.22)
Investment		0.0003**	0.0003**
		(2.27)	(2.01)
Kaufmann, Kraay and Z.-L.-Index	0.011***		0.011***
	(3.40)		(3.57)
Ethnic	**-0.007**	**-0.021****	**-0.006**
	(-0.77)	**(-2.48)**	**(-0.70)**
Immigration Dummy	-0.015***	-0.015***	-0.013 ***
	(-2.84)	(-2.76)	(-2.59)
Immigration*Ethnic	**0.023***	**0.026****	**0.021***
	(1.94)	**(2.05)**	**(1.83)**
Total Pool No. Obs.	282	336	280
Adj R2	0.41	0.35	0.39

Source: Own Calculations. Note: t-stats in parentheses *0.1, **0.05, ***0.01 Significance level.

Table 1.14: Indirect Effect of Fragmentation in Immigration Countries.

	Investment 1960-99	Investment 1960-99	Governance
Variable			
Dummy for the 1960s	-15.503	-3.932	5.239**
	(-0.64)	(-0.15)	(2.25)
Dummy for the 1970s	-15.196	-3.352	5.060**
	(-0.62)	(-0.12)	(2.17)
Dummy for the 1980s	-19.115	-6.684	4.898**
	(-0.79)	(-0.25)	(2.10)
Dummy for the 1990s	-20.176	-8.206	4.644**
	(-0.83)	(-0.30)	(2.00)
Dummy SSA	-1.781	-0.427	0.104
	(-1.12)	(-0.22)	(0.59)
Log of initial income	8.087	4.981	-1.741***
	(1.34)	(0.74)	(-3.04)
Log of initial income sq.	-0.333	-0.105	0.148***
	(-0.89)	(-0.25)	(4.191)
Openness	0.045***		
	(4.63)		
Dependency Ratio	-11.428***	-9.704**	
	(-3.01)	(-2.16)	
Ethnic	-3.961	-5.913*	-0.720**
	(-1.49)	(-1.85)	(-2.39)
Immigration Dummy	-5.259***	-5.742**	-0.164
	(-2.58)	(-2.31)	(-0.87)
Immigration*Ethnic	8.608**	10.763**	0.164
	(1.95)	(2.01)	(0.38)
Total Pool No. Obs.	380	415	316
Adj R2	0.53	0.41	0.71

Source: Own Calculations. Note: t-stats in parentheses *0.1, **0.05, ***0.01 Significance level.

To conclude this section, we find clear evidence that ethnic fractionalisation in immigration countries has a positive growth enhancing effect, which counteracts the measured negative effect of ethnic fractionalisation. This effect is found to be due to increased investments in the host country. In line with the argumentation of Acemoglu (2001), we can therefore confirm that migrants with a long-term perspective are more willing to productively engage and partly assimilate in their host country. Thus, the net effect of ethnic fractionalisation in immigration countries on economic performance and growth is positive and very different from the negative effect of multi-ethnic societies which might be suffering from historically entrenched, possibly rival, ethnic fractionalisation due to post-colonial border drawing.

1.6 Conclusion and Future Research Questions

In the end, interestingly, the transmission channels which explained how ethnic fractionalisation negatively affects growth, namely via policy variables, is less prominent in the extended analysis (using the updated dataset), as ethnic fractionalisation remains a significant negative explanatory power in the growth regression for Sub-Saharan African countries even after the inclusion of the policy variables. Thus, the negative impact of ethnic fractionalisation on economic growth cannot fully be explained by the model of Alesina et al. (2003). We find that a highly fractionalised society in Sub-Saharan Africa in which governments point at ethnic differences and instrumentalise ethnic differences to stay in power create a poor investment climate.

Moreover, as already mentioned above, there might be a further conceivable transmission channel of high ethnic fractionalisation on growth, namely income inequality. Especially, if one considers a longer time horizon, very high income inequality, which might be a result of high ethnic fractionalisation and segregation in connection with badly designed institutions, might lead to a reduction in growth via the suboptimal provision and accumulation of factors of production, such as physical and human capital. This explanation gains validity especially in countries with imperfect markets. A further inquiry into this matter seems very much worthwhile, but rather difficult to facilitate due to the limitation of useable cross-country data sources on income inequality.

Concerning migration, ethnic fractionalisation and growth, this paper suggests that there is a mitigating positive impact in countries which are characterised as immigration countries. This gives some further empirical validation to the theory of Acemoglu (2001). Promising future research in this field should focus on a new measure of fractionalisation that is sensitive to changes in fractionalisation through immigration. With this new measure the link between fractionalisation and the network enhancing trade effect of immigration in a country cross-section framework could be investigated. This would strengthen the argument above and confirm the case studies' findings on co-ethnic network theory in a wider setting.

In conclusion, this paper corrects the initial assessment that ethnic fractionalisation is exclusively one of the key determinants of a negative policy environment and subsequent poor growth performance. This is only the case in non-immigration countries, which might be suffering from historically entrenched, possibly rival, ethnic fractionalisation due to post-colonial border drawing. Furthermore, we put emphasis on the findings by Easterly (2001) which show that even in those countries, democratic institutions and low inequality can resolve ethnic conflict in the political sphere. Thus, countries with high ethnic fractionalisation and a strong income-divide between groups face the danger, but not necessarily the consequences of growth retardation. Hence, the challenge ahead, in particular in Sub-Saharan Africa, is the full participation of all ethnic groups in the economic development process and the blurring of ethnic ties, which might be a way to overcome this serious obstacle in many developing countries.

Chapter 2

Incentive Effects of Transfers within the Extended Family: The Case of Indonesia

2.1 Introduction

External remittances, defined as private financial transfers from abroad, are a major source of external financing in developing countries. According to the World Bank, external intra-family transfer flows to developing countries were estimated at 240 billion dollars in 2007 (World Bank, 2006 (1)). Similarly, internal intra-family transfer flows in many developing countries are substantial as well. Cox and Jimenez (1990) review studies on private internal intra-family transfers in developing countries. They find that 20-90 percent of households in developing countries receive private transfers, comprising 2-20 percent of household income. In the same time frame only 15 percent of households in the United States received such transfers, comprising only 1 percent of household income on average. Due to the high volume of external and internal intra-family transfers in developing countries, researchers have asserted their potentially positive impact on development. The literature has suggested that intra-family transfers could help to reduce poverty, help smooth household income, ease capital constraints and increase household expenditures in areas like education, health or entrepreneurship. On the other hand, one might expect that intra-family transfers trigger the same adverse incentive effects as public transfers.

This paper aims to further deepen the research on the economic effects of intra-family transfers. It will evaluate the concerns raised regarding the indirect effects of remittances on household income through changes to the labor supply. Very little research has been done on this issue to date, and development practitioners are only beginning to be concerned with the indirect impacts of remittances. Due to data availability this analysis concentrates on internal intra-family transfers. It is possible to translate the results on economic effects of internal remittances into the context of external remittances. Both are like any other form of cash/in-kind transfer received by the household. More common characteristics are shared by internal and external remittances. External remittances are associated with an even worse informational asymmetry between giver and recipient of the transfer.[1]

[1] Furthermore, as empirical studies like that of Adams (1996) show, the cost of international migration are higher. Therefore relatively more wealthy households send members abroad. These sending households also have in common that their labour market situation is likely to be better. This implies that endogeneity problems might be less severe. It is more unlikely that a situation occurs where a job loss or reduction in working hours draws remittances, than a situation where remittances lead to an reduction in working hours.

A number of studies point to reduced participation rates as a consequence of remittances (Itzigsohn, 1995; Funkhouser, 1992). The shortcoming of these studies is that they do not take the endogeneity of remittances into account. The only study so far controlling for endogeneity when examining the incentive effects of external remittances on working hours is that on Nicaragua of Andersen and Tejerina (2005). The contribution of this paper is to take into account endogeneity and evaluate the robustness of the results using different economic techniques.

In the Indonesian context, the research so far has investigated whether intra-family transfers act as an old-age support system and therefore as a substitute for the labor supply of elderly Indonesians. The information provided in the Indonesian Family Life panel data survey on migration and internal remittances is extremely rich and of high quality which is not found in any other survey to the knowledge of the author. Panel data on remittance flows are rare. The advantage of this data in addition to the panel character of the information is the symmetry of information about transfer givers and recipients and the amount of transfers in cash and in kind that flows from migrants to the household of origin and from the household of origin to migrants. This gives a more complete picture of transfer flows and allows to calculate the net amount of transfers received in a given year. The net amount might not only be important for evaluating incentive effects but also for analyzing welfare effects.

This paper differs from earlier studies considering incentive effects on the labor market in that it examines whether there exist adverse incentive effects of intra-family transfers on working hours rather than on labor market participation of the working age population. Theory does predict exit from the labor market but less exertion of effort and therefore a reduction of normal hours worked. Furthermore it is easier to condition a remittance contract on labor market participation since it might be possible to receive information of trusted witnesses.

The theoretical framework can be described shortly. Transfers cause a positive income effect and a possible income-smoothing effect. As a result of the income effect, if leisure is considered a normal good, more leisure will be consumed. Through the income-smoothing effect the household is insured against shocks. The better the household is insured the less incentive the household has to exert effort on avoiding a negative income shock. It might be, however, that the stream of transfers an individual receives over time is incentive-compatible in that it does not react to all household income shocks perfectly. In other words, if transfers do not provide perfect insurance, the disincentive is clearly reduced. In this case the household has to put in effort on his own in order to maximize the probability to be able to cover the cost of shocks. Due to the imperfectness of observability of effort between givers and recipients an incentive compatible contract is not possible.[2] Furthermore, the informational asymmetry between migrants and household members left behind makes it impossible to evaluate whether the recipient supplemented the insurance provided through the family network with formal or other informal insurance.[3]

Another contribution of the paper is to distinguish between different sectors of employment, which has not been done before. First of all, the

2 The sending household and the migrant live in different villages or even provinces.

3 The data presented and analyzed in Section 4 indicate that informal workers have access to other, non-family informal insurance schemes, as well.

formal and the informal labor market are analyzed separately. This is based on the indisputable fact that formal sector workers are less flexible in adjusting their working hours, and that the costs of doing so might be higher for them. Furthermore, there is the possibility of oppositional effects of transfers between sectors. Whether an individual works mainly in the subsistence agricultural or the non-agricultural sector has major implications on the impact of transfers. Migrants may restrict household production in agriculture since missing labor is difficult to replace in the agricultural sector (Rozelle, 1999). Furthermore, in rural areas credit market constraints might be more severe. Engagement in the non-farm sector might become possible through remittances. Rural areas, however, also face missing opportunities of non-farm engagement. Therefore it is unclear whether remittances can give the incentive to start working in the non-farm sector. More importantly, the relaxation of the credit constraint might lead to investment in better technology. This clarifies that a focus on working hours might be flawed. In the agricultural sector disincentive effects should instead be measured by investigating a potential reduction in productivity of the farm household.[4]

The results indicate that there exists an adverse incentive effect on work effort created by a positive net remittance flow. Results are robust to use of different measures of remittances. Considering the family members of working age as a whole this effect is significant in size. It is hard, however, to determine the reaction of which household member drives the result. Nevertheless the empirical analysis shows that remittances cause

[4] A negative sign of the variable "transfers" may more realistically imply the substitution of labor by more productive assets.

positive welfare effects at the household level by insuring the household at least partly against shocks.

This chapter is structured as follows. Section 2.2 provides a literature review on the allocation of remittances in general and incentive effects found in empirical research of public and private external or internal transfers. Section 2.3 will summarize the theory behind the empirical analysis. The general empirical analysis presented at the outset of Section 2.4 does not distinguish between different sectors. Subsection 2.4.5 presents the empirical findings for the different employment sectors. Section 2.5 concludes and outlines future research questions.

2.2 Literature Review

2.2.1 Motives for Transfers

Before reviewing the literature on the effects of transfers found, the theoretical and empirical evidence on the motives of transfer providers will be briefly reviewed. These motives may give some initial insight into the effects. Since altruistic or reciprocal motives are likely to generate transfers that insure the household, it could be hypothesized that these transfers are therefore more likely to produce negative incentive effects. Gatti (2005) however shows that this need not be the case.

Gatti (2005) hypothesizes that an altruistic motive of giving leads to perfect insurance of household members through migrants' transfers if there were no informational asymmetries between migrants and household members left behind. The more insurance is provided by migrants the less effort household members have to exert to avoid a shock. However, if the assumption of no informational asymmetries does not hold the picture changes. Gatti (2005) highlights that an incentive-compatible contract nevertheless is consistent with an altruistic motive of giving. She puts forward an incentive compatible pattern of transfers in an altruistic model of the family. Here, recipient's effort is endogenous and transfer providers only have imperfect information on recipient's income realizations. If transfer providers can credibly commit to a pattern of transfers, they will underinsure the recipient. Thus transfers react to shocks but do not fully cover the cost of shocks. Therefore the recipient household still has to put in effort to avoid the shock. Provider's money is not "wasted". When looking at one single extended family, transfers are higher for recipients with higher income than for those with lower income. If this is the case the disincentive effect of transfers should be rather small in size. The same model can be build with reciprocity as the underlying motive.

Empirically the insurance motive of remittance givers can be clearly found (Wolff et al., 2007; World Bank, 2007; Azam and Gubert, 2005). Little evidence has been found in the literature on the existence of purely altruistic transfer givers, that is givers that give without any self-interest.

Lucas and Stark (1985) question the idea that pure altruism can explain remittance behavior in the extended family. First, they hypothesize and indeed find empirical evidence that self-interest or egoism is an important motive. Competition for inheritances, for example, may explain why wealthier households receive more remittances. Second, they find that remittances may be motivated by the desire to return home without shame. Lucas and Stark‘s (1985) results also indicate that remittances are part of a loan contract with the family or reciprocal exchange: parents pay for their children's education and children in return remit resources to repay these costs.

A series of papers has analyzed the motives of transfers within the extended family using the Indonesia Family Life Surveys (IFLS), which are also used in this paper. Park (2003) estimates the motives separately for the parent-to-child, child-to-parent, and inter-sibling relationship using the first wave of the survey from 1993. His findings suggest that the parent-to-child relationship is driven by the motive of exchange for filial services, whereas children seem to provide old-age support to parents, and siblings seem to help mainly younger siblings who have less income and assets.[5]

Frankenberg et al. (2002) find that even transfers between parents and children cannot be explained by a single theory, but that three motives are consistent among them. Using the same survey data as Park (2003), their findings indicate that transfers may be a source of insurance, based on an educational loan contract, or an exchange for time. Raut and Tran (1998) use the same dataset as the aforementioned authors but find no evidence for the pure educational loan contract hypothesis, and interpret the results instead as pure reciprocity. The two motives are strongly alike.

Cameron and Cobb-Clark (2005) use the same IFLS 1993 dataset to investigate old-age support strategies of elderly Indonesians given the

[5] The shortcoming of a study such as Park's is that it does not take into account the transfer amount given by the recipient when analyzing the amount of transfers received by the recipient. Therefore the analysis is incomplete and it cannot be judged from the results whether altruism or reciprocity is the reason of giving.

lack of a public insurance scheme. They find little evidence that transfers from children or co-residence with children acts as a substitute for the elderly parents' need to work.

Transfer behavior, especially that between parents and children, generally seems to be determined by reciprocity. A reciprocal motive of giving is in line with an insurance motive of givers. Transfers might be part of a mutual insurance system between migrants and household members. This insurance motive of giving is in line with the following theoretical argument of disincentive effects of remittances which are the more pronounced the better the recipient is insured.

2.2.2 Incentive Effects of Transfers

One of the most well-known empirical studies demonstrating the disincentive effects of transfers is that of Bertrand et al. (2003). Under the South African pension program, the elderly receive cash transfers equal to roughly twice the average per capita income of Africans. The results indicate that prime-age individuals reduce their working hours significantly as a response to transfers received by the household. The authors also find that transfers cause the labor supply to decline. Klasen and Woolard (2005) find that households with access to state support attract unemployed relatives and that this household formation response draws away some unemployed from employment opportunities. Using the same data, Posel et al. (2006) additionally investigate the labor supply of household members who leave to find work. The authors find that rural African women are significantly more likely to be labor migrants if the household they belong to receives pensions. To sum up, disincentive effects are created through the attraction of unemployed to the household. However, only a part of prime-age adults are affected negatively. Females seem to use the increase in household income by investing in temporary migration to seek employment.

One of the first papers dealing with the topic of the economic effects of remittances is that of Funkhouser (1992). For Nicaragua he finds a negative effect of remittances on the probability to participate in the labor force. Concerning the employed he finds a higher probability to be self-employed for those who receive higher remittances. During the period under study, the author detects that migration took place not only for political reasons but also because of the worsening economic situation in Nicaragua. This implies that unemployment of a household member may be the reason for others to migrate and send remittances. This possible endogeneity of remittances is not considered, however.

Similarly, Itzigsohn's (1995) empirical results suggest that receiving remittances leads to a higher probability of not participating in the labor market. His analysis is based on 1991 data for Jamaica, Haiti and the Dominican Republic. The aim is to analyze whether remittances allow households to send fewer people into the labor market when unemployment is high or whether they simply allow people to avoid taking less desirable jobs. However, again, this argumentation and interpretation is questionable since the endogeneity of remittances is not controlled for. The endogeneity arises because the direction of causality can run in both ways. The involuntarily unemployed attract remittances and remittances may cause a voluntary withdrawal from the labor market.

A more recent analysis of the impact of remittances (internal as well as external remittances) in Nicaragua is the one of Andersen and Terjerina (2005). This study has the advantage of analyzing panel data over the years of 1998 and 2001 which can be characterized as a period of an economic upturn. Overall, average normal working hours per week rose between those years, but significantly less so for people receiving higher amounts of remittances in 1998. It might be nonetheless possible that those households that received higher amounts of transfers in the past are more disadvantaged in finding a regular employment or are even partly excluded from the economic boom. Andersen et. al. do not control for this possibility in their empirical analysis. Furthermore, Andersen and Terjerina (2005) do not state that they take into account a possible selection bias by including only households that received positive remittances in 1998.

Besides the paper of Andersen and Terjerina (2005), all aforementioned studies investigate the effect of remittances in a period of economic crisis. Thus even if panel data are available it is not clear whether the crisis or remittances drive the result. This paper will therefore also consider data that do not coincide with an overall economic downturn.

In developing countries credit markets are imperfect and remittances may therefore allow profitable investment that would otherwise not have been undertaken by households with little wealth (Woodruff et al., 2001). Woodruff et al. (2001) concentrate their analysis on urban areas. They seem to find some evidence on the aforementioned hypothesis in Mexico. Individuals born in states of Mexico characterized by high migration rates into the U.S., are more likely to own a micro-enterprise.[6] The effect found could also be driven by returning migrants that invest their savings rather than remittances.

Yang's (2005) panel analysis for the Philippines shows that positive transitory remittance shocks through currency appreciation coincide with an increase in hours worked in self-employment and are correlated with recipient households' entry into relatively capital-intensive enterprises. Furthermore, the positive income shock coincided with a reduction of child labor. Though the variable used to measure a positive remittance shock is clearly exogenous to labor supply, it might capture the effect of a positive macro- and meso-level development on household behavior instead of the intended effect of remittances.

Moreover, there is literature on the economic effects of migration and remittances in the agricultural sector. As Lucas (1987) shows, there can be two distinct effects of migration and remittances in rural areas. Migration may lead to a reduction in output in the short run, remittances however increase output in the long run by relaxing the capital constraint of households.

Rozelle et al. (1999) investigate the linkages between migration, remittances, and agricultural productivity using three-stage least squares. Household members who leave the farm may not be exchangeable because on-farm labor markets work imperfectly. Remittances may compensate for this foregone labor by releasing the capital constraint of the household. The authors conclude that migration and remittances exer-

[6] They were not able to analyze entry and into and exit from the micro-enterprise sector.

cise a negative net impact on maize production in rural northeast China. Some studies including Collier and Lal (1984, 1986) and Bates (1976) analyze only the compensating effect. They find that recipient families indeed hold more productive capital than others. Azam and Gubert (2005) emphasize that remittances act as an insurance contract in the extended family that may give rise to moral hazard. Their results suggest that recipients use productive resources significantly less efficiently than households without migrants. They do not, however, analyze the separate effect of foregone labor.

The recent evidence on the economic effect of migration and remittances in the agricultural sector puts Lucas' early results into question. Indeed recent studies find evidence of a negative incentive effect of remittances by creating moral hazard.

Overall the literature review indicates that economically significant disincentive effects of remittances in the non- as well as agricultural sector are prevailing. The migrant effect is no disincentive effect as such. It might capture a transition away from agriculture in developing countries, where the rural and urban non-farm sector is said to gain in importance.

2.3 Theoretical Framework - Intuition

The analysis presented in this paper focuses on internal remittances and less so on external remittances. The main difference between internal and external remittances is that the former more often flow in two directions, from migrants to the household of origin and the other way round.

Individuals can be assumed to be rational in the sense that they only consider the net amount of transfers they received when making decisions on labor supply. This assumption might be criticized because the provider's decision to give and the recipient's decision to give are made at two quite distinct points in time. However, if we consider the exchange of money as a repeated interaction[7] that took place over several years, then we can even assume that the recipient is well informed and is able to estimate the expected amount of net transfers he or she might receive. Migrants and left behind household members know the characteristics of each other quite well and can judge each others sensitivity to shocks. Furthermore household members learned in the past whether it is likely that a migrant will be successful given his/her characteristics.[8] It follows that using gross transfers is inappropriate for examining the incentive effect of internal remittances.[9] The descriptive statistics show that the transfer behavior did not change for a long time horizon. The behavior found in the 2000 wave is similar to that found in the 1993 wave. Therefore transfers can be interpreted as being part of a repeated interaction and that the household can anticipate net transfers. Nevertheless, the empirical analysis analyzes gross remittances also.

The standard economic theory on choices about hours of work tells us that a positive income effect leads to the consumption of more leisure

7 This assumption is clearly underlined by the data used. Migrants and the household of origin stay in contact over several years by transferring money.

8 Second, motives could differ between recipient and provider or between transfer providers. Therefore the model takes the observable characteristics of household members living outside the household into account. Even if there is no symmetry in motives the argument for using net transfers remains valid. The household does not care about the source of transfers and every transfer is a positive income shock.

9 Up to now the few studies using data on internal remittance flows do not indicate or discuss the use of net transfers. In many surveys, transfers given are not available.

if leisure is considered a normal good. Additionally there may exist an distorting substitution effect if transfers are conditioned on low income of the recipient (World Bank, 2006 (2)). If the transfer is conditioned on low income, the more the transfer insures the household against the low-income state of the world, the less the incentive of the household to put effort into the avoidance of the event.

Several informational asymmetries exist between migrants and the families they leave behind (Azam and Gubert, 2002). Migrants cannot observe the effort level of left-behind household members perfectly. The effort level determines the likelihood that a future shock causes a severe drop in household income. Migrants can get a general impression through trusted witnesses[10] or by comparing the family's material outcome with neighbors, which as well can be observed only imperfectly. Thus, they cannot use credible threats to punish shirking. Imperfect monitoring produces an incentive to lower effort. This incentive is higher the more reliable the insurance that is provided by transfers. Insurance is provided by potential transfers the household may receive as well. Potential transfers are measured by the number of family members not residing in the household. Uncertainty about the behavior of migrants might reduce the disincentive. Migrants may be an unreliable source of transfers as they may lie about their own financial situation.[11] Shirking by migrants themselves might be rather unlikely since they do not want to lose face in front of their family and want to be able to return home without shame.

[10] A trusted witness will most likely be a family member or friend living near by. In which case it is not in his interest to prove the information given by the family of origin wrong.

[11] Therefore the household might send more migrants in order to be sure that at least some will send transfers.

It seems plausible to assume that migrants receive a positive utility from sending home money. This is especially the case if internal migrants are considered mainly. These might have closer links to their families and face a lower cost to return home.[12]

Migrants are also likely to be petitioners themselves. What follows is that the disincentive effect of internal transfers could work in both directions, in the direction of household of origin and in the direction of migrants. This is due to the informational asymmetry on both sides, as explained above. The motive of sending away migrants again is important here. If the motive is for the migrants to look for an employment or take advantage of better opportunities somewhere else, more transfers flow from migrants to the household of origin in all likelihood. If so, it makes sense to analyze disincentive effects on the household. If the motive is to send migrants in order to enable better education, remittances are more likely to flow in the other direction. For this reason the remittance relationship of the households in Indonesia have to be described before analyzing potential disincentive effects.[13]

This paper analyzes the effects of transfers on the incentive to work. Due to informational asymmetries transfers can be conditioned on participation in the labor market but not on the effort level, that is, the number of hours worked in the job. It is more easy for migrants to observe labor market participation through trusted witnesses than working hours of members of the household of origin. If a transfer contract conditioned

12 If instead a migrant does not plan to return from abroad the incentive to transfer (regularly) might be significantly lowered.

13 To the knowledge of the author working hours and labor supply of migrants in general are often not available in surveys.

on working hours were possible, there would be no disincentive. Moreover, it is important to bear in mind that the negative effect on working hours will only be observable if the household is able to survive without remittances. If cash and in-kind transfers received by others supplement household income in a way that this **just** guarantees survival, there is less incentive to lower work effort as this would lead to a situation where the household would have to struggle for survival.

The positive income shock might not be exogenous to the opportunities the household has to participate in the labor market. In order to separate the effects of opportunities and income shocks the empirical model needs to instrument for income shocks, and control for neediness and opportunities.

No matter whether the transfer is given due to lack of a job or to a limited amount of opportunities, there could nevertheless exist negative effects on incentives. These could adversely affect household members' efforts to look for a new job or a better paid job, or to simply work more hours. As explained above, this is conditioned on the insurance the transfer provides.

A straightforward application of this model would be the informal non-agricultural labor market. In the informal labor market labor supply decisions are very flexible whereas in the formal labor market this is not the case. Furthermore, households working in subsistence agriculture might struggle for survival even if they receive remittances. In rural areas, there are fewer opportunities to engage in the non-farm sector. However, remittances might be used to invest in a better technology. Therefore the focus on working hours might not be justifiable in the agricultural sector. Here, disincentive effects could result in lower productivity even if better technology is used.

Furthermore, we would expect quite distinct effects of the number of migrants sent away in the agricultural sector. Migrants may constrain the household's production as missing labor cannot be easily replaced in the agricultural sector. The more migrants the household sends away, the more the remaining members need to work.

As in most developing countries a large fraction of the Indonesian population is active in the informal labor market. In such a society, transfers through family networks should play an important role. The Indonesian Family Life Survey data from 2000 additionally show that other informal insurance schemes are existent and widely used in the society. Thus, the possibility of overinsurance, that is topping up the (incentive-compatible) family insurance through transfers with other insurance, exits in both the formal and the informal sector.

To sum up, informational asymmetries lead to an incentive to shirk that results most likely in a reduction of working hours. This will only occur if the household is not credit- and at the same time opportunity-constrained.

2.4 Empirical Analysis

2.4.1 Description of the Data

The empirical analysis is based on the Indonesian Family Life Surveys 1 and 3 (IFLS), a panel survey representative of 83 percent of the Indonesian population living in 13 of the 26 Indonesian provinces in 1993. The first wave collected detailed information on individuals living in 7,224 households. The third wave of 2000 tried to re-interview the entire 1993 sample. The second wave of the panel survey from 1997 cannot be used because the employment data still have not been released. Due to high re-contact rates of 95.3 percent the possible problem of non-random attrition is relatively low. 6,564 households or 90.9 percent of the IFLS 1 sample were interviewed in all three waves.

The wave of 2000 and that of 1993 collects detailed information on the transfers a household received or provided, and the insurance status and employment characteristics of household members. The data on transfers consist mainly of transfers to and from migrants inside of Indonesia. Only very few households indicated that family members migrated to other countries. International remittances therefore make up only a minor part of the transfer data collected.

The subject of analysis of this study is the working behavior of household members of working age. Detailed data was collected on the characteristics of migrants, which are the children, parents and siblings of these couples that live outside the household.

The analysed panel sample consists of 4278 households that answered the section on non-coresiding household members and the employment section. Households that indicated that some of the children, siblings and/or parents of the head and spouse of the household live outside of the head's and/or spouse's household in 1993 and/or 2000 are included in the sample.[14]

2.4.2 Method of Analysis

The availability of panel data makes a first difference approach a natural starting point of analysis:

$$\triangle W_{i,t-(t-1)} = \alpha + \beta \triangle T_{i,t-t-1} + \gamma \triangle \mathbf{X}_{i,t-t-1} + u_i, where$$

$\triangle W_i$ is the change in normal hours worked per week between 2000 and 1993[15] of the i-th household. It is defined as the sum of normal hours worked of all household members of working age. $\triangle T_i$ measures the change in remittances between 2000 and 1993 this household receives. It is complicated to control for endogeneity in such a setting. It is unclear whether the decrease in working hours draws transfers or whether the increase in remittances leads to a reduction in working hours. Therefore it would be important to instrument for the change in remittances and estimate the model using two-stage least squares. The advantage would be that we would explicitly model and estimate the effect of a change in remittances on a change in working hours. The inclusion of $\triangle T_{i,t-1}$ could solve the endogeneity problem. The second wave of the survey , however, can not be used to construct such an instrument. The data

[14] The analysis therefore does not consider explicitely households that send away temporary or permanent migrants. It is instead considering all households that can be characterized by non-coresiding relatives (children, siblings, parents) of the head and spouse.

[15] Note again that the 1997 employment data is not yet released.

are influenced by the crisis that took place in 1997 in Indonesia. Some regions were exposed to a severe draught. Inflation of food prices affected nearly all households. It is therefore clear that such a covariant shock led to a decline in remittances. Therefore I will follow a second-best approach. The initial level of remittances in 1993 is used to predict the change in working hours between 1993 and 2000. The higher the initial level of remittances, the more the household reduces working hours in the future.

$$\triangle W_{i,t-(t-1)} = \alpha + \beta T_{i,t-1} + \gamma \mathbf{X}_{i,t-1} + u_i, \mathit{where}$$

$T_{i,t-1}$ is the initial level of remittances received by the household in 1993 and $\mathbf{X}_{i,t-1}$ is a vector of other household characteristics in 1993. This approach can reduce the endogeneity problem to at least some extent. If it is true that missing opportunities and vulnerability of a household are positively correlated over time and additionally positively correlated with (net) remittances, then the initial level of remittances is not exogenous to the change in working hours. This critique can only be tackled by trying to include variables in the model that should absorb or be highly correlated with the above mentioned meso- or macro characteristics that determine the change in working hours. Therefore variables that measure the proneness to shocks and exclusion from opportunities are included in the regression model.

The model is tested for the household as a whole. It is tested as well for the head and its spouse of working age, because they are the ones controlling household resources. To know whether working-age children, siblings or parents of the household head and spouse show behavioral changes, the model is also tested for these subgroups. It should again be pointed out that the survey provides mainly information on internal migration and internal remittances. Therefore a sample selection bias that could potentially be generated by only looking at those households with international migrants is non-existent. Virtually all households indicate that a close relative of head or spouse lives outside their household. The empirical model can be described as follows:

$$\triangle W_{i,t-(t-1)} = \alpha + \beta_1 \mathbf{X}_{i,t-1} + \beta_2 T_{t-1} + \beta_3 S_{t-1} + \varepsilon_i$$

$\triangle W_i \equiv \triangle$normal working hours per week of head/spouse/household (sum)

$\mathbf{X}_{i,t-1} \equiv$ Characteristics of the head/spouse/household in t-1

$\mathbf{T}_{t-1} \equiv$ Remittances per head received in t-1

$\mathbf{S}_{t-1} \equiv$ Shocks experienced by the household prior to t

A crucial point is to decide on the measure of internal transfers. Even if theory and also the data indicate that households repeatedly interact, it seems reasonable to check whether the results hold using gross transfers. However, using gross remittances can lead to a sample selection bias. Households receiving gross transfers might be very different from households giving remittances, particularly concerning working hours. The same complication arises when using positive net transfers as a measure of transfers received. Assigning each household with negative or zero net transfers a zero might further distort the data analyzed. Why not using net remittances? Theory does not predict a symmetry of effects of positive compared to negative net transfers on working hours. This is because a rich household is "rich" enough to give and will not have to increase working hours in the future due to on balance giving transfers. Theory does predict a symmetry of effects between well-insured and under-insured households. Insurance is provided through remittances and might be even topped up, as explained above. If the household is under-insured household members of working age have to exert effort in form of working more hours (in an additional job or by the entry of one more member into the economically active population), to cope with the shock and possible future shocks. Another possible measure of transfers is a Dummy variable which takes the value of zero for all households with zero or negative net transfers and a value of one for all others. A potential sample selection bias is avoided.

Another source of misspecification can result from the use of gross remittances. The amount of gross remittances is expected to be positively related to household income. The share of remittances in household income could be used as a measure instead. But as, for good reasons presented above, the analysis concentrates on net remittances, the relationship between remittances and income is unclear. Richer households might receive more, but also give more. Furthermore, using the share of remittances in household income creates a problem. Household income and working hours are positively correlated. This measure therefore creates a negative correlation between the income share of remittances and working hours by definition.

Due to the aforementioned critique on the approach, the data are also analyzed in the cross-section using the 2000 wave. The analysis focuses on head and spouse, as the first difference approach showed unclear results for this sub-sample of the household. In the cross-section, theory would predict lower working hours for individuals or households that receive higher remittances. A three-stage least squares approach is deemed the best estimation technique in order to control for endogeneity.

Three basic equations shape the empirical model. First of all, normal hours worked W of the household head or his/her spouse of working age in 2000 are modeled as a function of the positive income shock the household encountered and the potential insurance provided by non-coresident family members (T and M). Given that the effect of T on normal hours worked in the formal or informal sector is to be determined, only individuals holding a job other than unpaid family work with positive working hours are included in the analysis. The set of characteristics of head and spouse that determine ability and neediness is denoted as vector **X**. The characteristics of coresiding family members are denoted as vector **Xc**. These determine the need to work.[16] The need to work is further controlled for by the variables of asset value per capita owned by the household and non-labor income per capita denoted as **I**. Furthermore, opportunities to work are proxied by the household's assessment whether poor people present in the village are poor mainly due to a lack

[16] Income earned by other household members could also be included in the regression. Theoretically these transfers are totally different to remittances. Transfers received by the head from within the household do not cause any disincentive effects. This is because no moral hazard problem is existent due to perfect information of co-residing family members. The effect of household income earned by other household members on working hours of the head/spouse is positive and significant. Results are not reported here.

of opportunities or for other reasons. This dummy variable is denoted as V. Unfortunately, no other more objective measure of opportunities is available.

$$W_i = \alpha + \beta_1 \mathbf{X}_i + \beta_2 \mathbf{Xc} + \beta_3 \mathbf{I} + \beta_4 V + \beta_5 T + \beta_6 M + \varepsilon_i \qquad (2.1)$$

$W_i \equiv$ normal working hours per week of individual i

Endogenous to this model are two variables: positive internal net transfers and the number of household members that migrated. Remittances may be endogenous because it is not the household members' decision on working hours that is driven by the amount of remittances received, but the decision of the donor to give due to reported missing opportunities of the recipient.

The number of migrants is also endogenous to working hours. Two forms of migration have to be distinguished. First, migrants may generate positive net remittances. Firstly, an individual with few or risky opportunities to work may decide to send some household members away to find better opportunities elsewhere. The more migrants the household has, the likelier the household may receive positive net transfers and the higher the amount of net transfers received. The neediness of a household may therefore determine the number of household members sent away from home. Secondly, the more household members are living outside the household, the more transfers the household itself might have to give. If this is the case the head or his/her spouse has to work in order to finance the transfers. Wealthier households will let household members migrate not for reasons of indigence, but for reasons of better opportunities of employment and education elsewhere. Theory calls this type demand-pull migration. In the latter case households may more likely be characterized by negative net transfers.[17] The reasons why household members migrate will be jointly driven by the two described motives. Most households in the sample receive and give transfers at the same time (see the next section).

In-kind and in-cash internal intra-family transfers[18] are produced by allowing family members to migrate. Given migration, the amount of net transfers received is influenced by household characteristics **X** that also affect the success of migrants and the motivation to return transfers. **Xnc** are characteristics of non-coresiding family members, measuring their ability to return transfers. **S** is a vector of shocks that hit the household in the last five years. The instrument Z in equation (2) is the amount of positive net transfers received from siblings in year 1993. It is used to identify equation (2) and is not correlated with the residuals of equation (1).[19]

$$T_j = \alpha + \beta_7 \mathbf{X}_{ij} + \beta_8 \mathbf{Xnc} + \beta_9 \mathbf{S} + \beta_{10} M + \beta_{11} Z + \varepsilon_j \qquad (2.2)$$

17 Here these households is assigned zero positive net transfers for the reason of avoiding a sample selection bias.

18 The empirical analysis presented here uses positive net transfers as dependent variable. The model was also run using gross transfers received. The coefficient of gross transfers is still negative, however not significant anymore, in the working hours regression.

19 The instrument that identifies the transfer regression is not significant if included in the working hour's regression.

$T \equiv$ ln of positive net transfers per capita, zero otherwise of household j

Note that positive net transfers are logarithmized to prevent the influence of outliers on the results.[20]

The number of household members that migrated in 2000 can be explained by household characteristics **X** and wealth status **I**. The wealthier a household the more migrants can be sent away. The older the head of the household the fewer other members will be sent away, as the need for assistance in the household increases with age. The number of migrants in 1993 are used to identify equation (3). This can be done due to the large time horizon considered. The number of migrants changed between 1993 and 2000. The correlation coefficient is 0.78. Therefore the migrants counted in 2000 are not a completely redundant measure of migrants counted in 1993. Furthermore the instrument is not correlated with residuals of equation (1) and (2).[21]

$$M_j = \alpha + \beta_{12}\mathbf{X} + \beta_{13}\mathbf{I} + \beta_{14}Z + \varepsilon_j \qquad (2.3)$$

$M \equiv$ number of close relatives living outside couple's hh

The error terms of the three equations are assumed to have zero mean, to have constant variances, and to be independently distributed following

[20] Even if some very high values of positive net remittances are thrown out of the sample the results do not change at all.

[21] The instrument that identifies the migrant regression is not significant if included in the working hour's regression and transfer regression.

the three-stage least squares method introduced by Zellner and Theil (1962). In this system of equations, however, it is possible that the error terms are correlated across equations (1) to (3). This is because all three dependent variables are exposed equally to the shocks a household faces. Therefore iterative three-stage least squares should be used to estimate the model.[22] Before presenting the results of the empirical models, the next section gives an overview of the data used for analysis.

Nevertheless, the three-stage least squares approach is deemed to be more unreliable when assessing the disincentive effects of transfers. This is because it is complicated to find statistical sound instruments that also make sense from the point of view of economic theory.

2.4.3 Descriptive Statistics

The empirical analysis uses a panel dataset. The sample consists of all households which were interviewed in the year 1993 and 2000 and whose head and spouse indicate to have parents non-coresiding and/or non-coresiding siblings and/or non-coresiding children. Tables B.1 (see appendix C) and 2.1 give an overview of the characteristics of couples and family members living outside of this household. Tables B.2 (see appendix C) and 2.2 describe the transfer behavior in 1993 and 2000.

The first row in Table B.1 (see appendix C) and 2.1 gives the average number of children, of siblings, and of parents coresiding and non-

22 The model presented here controls extensively for the shocks the household encountered. The questionnaires of IFLS 2000 and 1993 asked whether the household experienced the death of a household member, the sickness of a household member, crop loss, a natural disaster, a business or job loss, or a decrease in household income. Furthermore the household was asked whether it was negatively affected by the Indonesian economic crisis of 1998.

Table 2.1: Characteristics of Householders and Non-Coresiding (NC) Family Members, 2000

	Relatives of Head/Spouse coresiding and non-coresiding						
	Head/Spouse	Children hh	Children nc	Siblings hh	Siblings nc	Parents hh	Parents nc
Average number per household	1.7	1.7	1	0	7	0	1.6
Percentage married	80	8.5	81	11	74	17	.
Percentage not yet married	6	89	16.5	73	17	0	.
Average Age	43	13	33	30	70	68	59.5
Percentage with							
primary education	46	35	46	34	47	37	45
secondary education	31	31	38	49	31	5	0
tertiary education	8	4.5	8	10	5	0	1
Females as a percentage of nc			51		49		60
Percentage out of province			22		25		0.5
Percentage working	65	11	66	6	66	4	60
Av. working hours per week j1	42	41		44		32	
Av. working hours per week j2	23	24		27		17	

Source: Own Calculations.
Note: Table presents average values.
Columns 3 to 8 sort the relatives of couples according to place of residence.
nc=non-coresiding, hh=household.

coresiding in 2000 and 1993. In general it can be seen that, parents did not live in the same household as their (adult) children and siblings did not live in the same household as their peers in both years. Of these individuals who were no longer residing with family members, 22 percent of the children, 25 percent of the siblings and 0.5 percent of the parents had moved out of the province by 2000. Children and siblings in the household of the couples were younger than those living outside the household. In contrast, parents outside the household were on average younger. Apparently they tend to move in with their children in old-age. Children who do not co-reside are older and therefore have a higher education on average than those who co-reside. In 1993 the same was true for parents non-coresiding. As expected the better educated individuals live outside the household. On the other hand, a higher percentage of siblings co-residing has completed higher education compared to siblings non-coresiding. This may be due to high indirect and direct costs of education, which are more easily borne if one can share the cost of living. Females make up a quite large fraction of non-coresidents: in the year 2000, they make up 51 percent of non-coresiding children, 49 percent of non-coresiding siblings and 60 percent of non-coresiding parents. They seem to move out of the household with marriage. More interesting is the employment situation of non-coresiding family members: 66 percent of the children and siblings and 60 percent of the parents who had migrated are employed.

Tables B.2 and 2.2 describe the transfer behavior of all households whose head and spouse have non-coresiding close relatives. In the year 2000 most transactions take place between siblings, as was the case in in 1993. In contrast to 1993 parents no longer play a role in transfers in 2000. The importance of children declines between 1993 and 2000. The 2000 survey indicates that 35.5 percent of the couples are net transfer recipients and 39 percent are net transfer providers.[23] This shows the importance of looking at net rather than gross transfer flows. 25 percent indicate that they do not receive and provide transfers though relatives live in a different household.

There is a large discrepancy between the mean and the median of net transfers received. Transfers vary widely overall. This gap between mean and median is however not due to one or few outliers. Other studies have also found a highly variable pattern of transfers. For the empirical analysis the original data are therefore transformed by taking the natural logarithm of the original values. Figure 1 shows that after the transformation the distribution of transfers does not exhibit outliers anymore. In the median, households receive positive net transfers of 194 US Dollar (PPP adjusted) in 2000 and the mean amount is 767 US Dollar (PPP adjusted). As a percentage of income, this results in a median percentage of 7.5 percent and a mean percentage of 62 percent. Thus households receive a significant amount of income through transfers.

It is of interest, furthermore, to compare average normal hours worked in 2000 of those working-age heads and spouses living in households that received positive, negative, and zero net transfers in 1993. This gives a first insight into the relationship between transfers and working hours, but causality is unclear. In the year 2000, the mean for heads with zero

[23] The other couples did not receive or provide transfers even though some of their close relatives live outside the household.

Table 2.2: Transfer activities and flows 2000 PPP USD

received and/or given to	All	Children	Siblings	Parents
Percentage of households who:				
receive or give transfers	78	18	76	0.6
receive transfers only	16	7	14	0
both receive and give transfers	42	8	37	0.1
give transfers only	19	3	20	0.4
on balance receive net transfers	35.5			
on balance give net transfers	39			
on balance receive/give zero	25			
Transfer flows:				
Mean net transfers received	104	-1	106	-1
Mean per capita household income	3372			
Mean per capita household asset value	8212			
Median net transfers received	0	0	0	0
Median per capita household income	947			
Median per capita household asset value	2808			
Net transfers:				
Percentage of households with positive net receipts	35.5	12	28.5	0.1
Median amount received	194	129.5	162.5	39
Mean amount received	767	383	797	39
Median percentage of income	5	3	4.5	2
Mean percentage of income	11	10	11	2
Percentage receiving less than 10 percent of income	55	58.5	59	86
Percentage receiving more than 50 percent of income	14	13	12.5	0
Number of households in overall categories	2991	527	2263	17
Source: Own calculations				

Note: The category "All" includes all households with non-coresiding children, sibling and parents (relatives of head or spouse). Children, siblings and parents are non-coresiding relatives of head or spouse. The categories "Children", "Siblings" and "Parents" include only those households with children, siblings or parents non-coresiding. The category "All" displays higher percentages than the subcategories Children, Siblings, Parents since households may be doing transfers to several groups. households with negative net transfers not reported here.

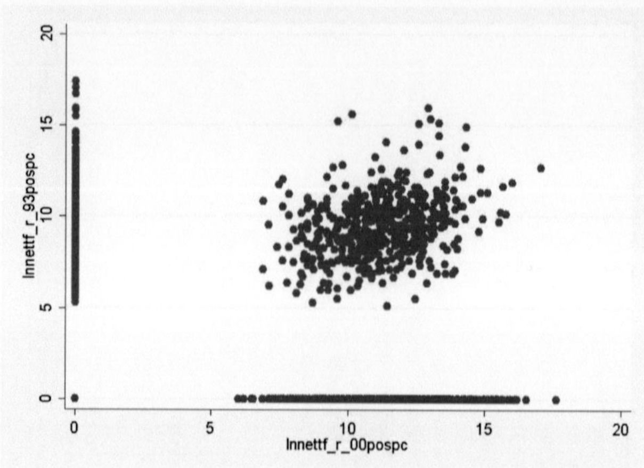

Figure 2.1: Natural logarithm of net positive transfer received 1993 and 2000

net transfers is given by an average of 44 hours worked normally per week, that of individuals with negative net transfers (net givers) is also 44 hours, and that of those with positive net transfers (net recipients) is 42 hours. Furthermore average normal working hours increase the least for heads and spouses which receive positive net transfers in 1993. The average change in normal working hours given the change in positive net remittances is also informative. The normal hours worked of those with an increase in positive net transfers drop by one hour, while the normal hours worked of those experiencing no change in net transfer increases and of those with a decrease in positive net transfers increases as well.

For the household as a whole normal working hours per week increase between 1993 and 2000 on average by 22 hours. This might be due to increased opportunities to work for the household members, partly to children which have not been of working age in 1993, and partly to a change in the structure of the household, meaning the group of individuals forming the household. The increase in labor supply is the lowest for households that receive positive net transfers in 1993 with a change by 19 hours. It is the highest for those receiving zero net transfers (23 hours) and slightly lower for those receiving negative net transfers in 1993 (22 hours). No such clear picture evolves when looking at the change in positive net transfers.

Table 2.3: Change in working hours and transfers

	working hours (2000)		*change in working hours*	
	head/spouse	household	head/spouse	household
net transfers (1993)				
positive	42	75	0.4	19
zero	44	79	3	23
negative	44	83	3	22
change in net transfers				
increase			-1	22
constant			5	21
decrease			4	21
Source: Own Calculations.				

Note: These are working hours or changes in working hours of individuals of working age.

2.4.4 Results

First Differences Approach

As theory does not clearly predict whether there might be a difference in the size and existence of disincentive effects between the head and his/her spouse and other co-residing household members, the model is also tested for the household as a whole.[24] The following regressions were also run using transfers per head (gross and net) as an explanatory variable. The results do not change when using this measure of transfers.[25]

Table 2.4[26] presents the results if the unit of observation is the whole household. The dependent variable of the regressions is the change in

[24] One can argue that the head and his/her spouse are the ones being the best informed of household resources available and can most completely dispose of household resources. Therefore it might be especially them that have the incentive to exert less effort given a positive income shock.

[25] The results can be received from the author upon request.

[26] Residual plots are shown in appendixB in Figures B.1 to B.5. The plots show that heteroscedasticity seems to be problematic. Therefore White-corrected standard errors were calculated.

Table 2.4: First Differences - Normal Hours Worked per Week Household Level - Robustness

	Dependent variable: change in normal hours worked per week				
in. pos. gross transfers p.c.	-2.554 (4.04)***				
initial net transfers p.c.		-0.186 (2.07)**			
in. pos. net transfers p.c.			-2.030 (2.56)**	-0.518 (3.06)***	
Dummy in. positive net tf					-4.095 (2.45)**
non-labor income	-0.115 (0.52)	-0.251 (1.53)	-0.502(1.80)*	-0.215 (1.31)	-0.228 (1.39)
asset value	-0.371 (0.66)	-0.769 (2.05)**	-0.403 (0.58)	-0.730 (1.96)*	-0.734 (1.97)**
rural	-12.637 (5.47)***	-12.818 (7.65)***	-11.217 (3.74)***	-12.887 (7.72)***	-12.848 (7.69)***
age	-0.437 (4.58)***	-0.360 (4.68)***	-0.382 (3.27)***	-0.354 (4.61)***	-0.361 (4.70)***
female	-7.290 (2.02)**	-8.991 (3.14)***	-5.843 (1.33)	-8.964 (3.13)***	-9.137 (3.19)***
perc. primary education	44.644 (7.82)***	49.608 (11.61)***	45.684 (6.08)***	49.203 (11.50)***	49.439 (11.56)***
perc. secondary education	61.215 (8.39)***	65.713 (11.80)***	58.272 (6.48)***	65.560 (11.79)***	65.593 (11.79)***
perc. tertiary education	112.600 (3.08)***	92.488 (3.82)***	85.971 (1.58)	91.884 (3.78)***	92.187 (3.79)***
opportunities	12.120 (5.43)***	9.670 (5.66)***	9.469 (3.23)***	9.729 (5.69)***	9.739 (5.70)***
shock prior to 1993	-10.192 (2.00)**	-11.256 (2.95)***	-16.327 (3.05)***	-11.099 (2.91)***	-11.130 (2.91)***
normal working hours 1993	-0.633 (-19.28)***	-0.619 (-25.73)***	-0.598 (-13.04)***	-0.619 (-25.75)***	-0.619 (-25.73)***
constant	85.955 (8.70)***	65.526 (11.25)***	78.844 (6.45)***	66.546 (11.40)***	66.592 (11.39)***
Number of observations	2364	4277	1280	4277	4277
Adj. R-squared	0.20	0.19	0.18	0.19	0.19

Source: Own calculations

T-statistic in parenthesis. Note:*0.1, **0.05, ***0.01 Significance level.

Table 2.5: First Differences - Normal Hours Worked per Week - Subgroup Analysis

Dependent variable: change in normal hours worked per week

1993-2000	(1-1)	(1 - 2)	(1-3)	(2)
	Head/Spouse	Head/Spouse	Head/Spouse	Children of working-age
asset value	-0.111 (0.22)	-0.057 (0.20)	-0.060 (0.21)	-0.051 (-0.12)
non-labor income	-0.104 (0.48)	-0.173 (1.40)	-0.169 (1.37)	-0.255 (-1.34)
positive net transfers 1993	-0.576 (0.92)	-0.228* (1.71)	-0.238* (1.79)	-1.297 (-2.38)**
rural	2.628 (1.12)	1.499 (1.17)	1.429 (1.11)	-6.308 (-3.12)***
age of head 1993	-1.015*** (9.72)	-0.891*** (14.04)	-0.881*** (13.85)	0.400 (5.23)***
female head	3.873 (1.15)	3.575 (1.64)	3.830* (1.75)	3.470 (1.24)
primary education head 1993	1.065 (0.35)	0.612 (0.33)	0.650 (0.35)	
secondary education head 1993	2.166 (0.56)	1.538 (0.70)	1.447 (0.66)	
tertiary education head 1993	1.369 (0.21)	2.054 (0.61)	1.925 (0.57)	
poor due to no opportunities	1.182 (0.46)	1.415 (1.00)	1.376 (0.97)	7.761 (3.48)***
household shocks:				
shock prior to 1993	-9.968* (1.96)	-3.967 (1.25)	-4.052 (1.28)	-6.470 (-1.45)
characteristics of m. co-residing				
percentage primary education	5.969 (1.11)	8.422*** (2.66)	8.649*** (2.73)	43.707 (9.24)***
percentage secondary education	8.124 (1.17)	12.261*** (3.08)	12.526*** (3.15)	52.070 (8.89)***
percentage tertiary education	6.227 (0.19)	15.897 (1.13)	16.436 (1.17)	106.206 (3.89)***
Normal working hours 1993			-0.161** (2.00)	-0.886 (-6.38)***
constant	42.920*** (4.32)	33.387*** (6.80)	33.179*** (6.75)	-2.667 (-0.32)
Number of observations	1174	3968	3968	1280
Adjusted R-squared	0.10	0.06	0.06	0,17

Source: Own calculations

T-statistic in parenthesis. Note:*0.1, **0.05, ***0.01 Significance level.

Note: The second specification (1-2) use only those households receiving positive net transfers. The first specification assigns households with negative or zero positive net transfers a zero for positive net transfers.

normal working hours per week between the years 2000 and 1993. Working hours are the sum of working hours of all individuals of working-age living in the household. I do not consider the "working hours" of those who indicated to be engaged in unpaid homework. A significant negative effect of all measures of transfers on the household's normal hours worked is found in all specifications. The results are robust to the inclusion of normal working hours in 1993 in the regression. From the descriptive statistics we know that working hours for the household as a whole increased, the least so for households having received positive net transfers in the past. Those households seem to have less incentive to increase working hours because they received income through other sources.

Those households that received positive net transfers in 1993 might be disadvantaged in opportunities to work compared to other households. Therefore the regressions include a dummy for whether the household experienced a shock in the years prior to 1993 that led to a decrease in household income due to a natural disaster or other macro/meso-type shock.[27] Furthermore, the variable "poor due to no opportunities" indicates whether the majority of inhabitants of the village or town is of the opinion that the poor stay poor due to no opportunities in the village or town to overcome poverty. This variable should capture opportunities available to the household. The positive and significant effect of it on the change in working hours indicates that households living in those villages seem to exert even more effort through an increase in working hours. The existence of shocks is significant in determining the change

[27] I consider shocks prior to 1993 as shocks in 1993 are highly correlated with transfers received in 1993.

in hours worked. Having experienced a shock detrimental to household income in the past goes along with a significantly less increase in working hours. Nevertheless the criticism on endogeneity of net transfers cannot be rejected fully.

Furthermore, the results show that a higher percentage of educated individuals in the household in 1993 the higher the increase in working hours. This is driven partly by the entry of household members into the labor force that were inactive in 1993. Moreover, participation in an economic upswing might take the form of resuming an additional job (inside the company or in another firm) and not by finding a job that is better paid.

The finding that the change in working hours was lower for those with higher initial working hours might indicate convergence. Normal working hours per week cannot be extended to infinity. Therefore it seems plausible that this result does not indicate measurement error but convergence of normal hours worked per week.

The following regression are individual-level regressions concentrating on the head and his/her spouse. Specification (1) and (1-2) differ in the measure used for positive net transfers in 1993. The former specification concentrates on households with positive net transfers only. The explanation power of the regression can be increased significantly through the inclusion of normal hours worked in 1993. A significant and negative effect of net transfers on normal hours worked is found in specification (1-3). A further individual-level specification was tested without females. Including normal working hours in 1993 renders the variable of positive net transfers insignificant. This table presents also evidence that normal hours worked of children of working-age living in the household are reduced through remittances. This might indicate that children are able to stay in school or university if the household gets assistance. These individual-level regressions are, however, not robust to the use of other measures for the positive income shock, besides the use of gross remittances received.

Overall, the presented results show that remittances seem to have indeed a negative effect on the work incentive of the household. The size of the effect ranges from a mean reduction of 0.2 to 2 in the household's normal working hours per week triggered by a one percent increase in remittances depending on the measure of net transfers used. Correcting for inflation, positive net remittances increased by 40 percent in the median between the two years. This has therefore approximately led to a decrease of 8 to 80 hours worked per week at the aggregate household level.This figure is a pure approximation and should be interpreted cautiously. It is not directly tested in the regression model. The level, not the change in transfers is used as explanatory variable due to the aforementioned endogeneity problems. Normal hours worked of the household as a whole increased from an average of 58 hours in 1993 to an average of 80 hours in 2000. The effective disincentive created is therefore severe. This estimate might not represent the true dynamic effect since it only measures the static effect of a certain difference in transfers received between households on the change in normal hours worked. The evidence on behavioral effects for the head and spouse are mixed. A different approach is therefore used to analyze this case more deeply.

Three-Stage Least Squares Approach

Because the explanatory power of the model for the year 2000 cannot be judged using 3SLS, ordinary least squares regressions were run to evaluate the explanatory power. The sample investigated includes all heads and spouses of working-age that work and have sent away migrants. Results are reported in table B.5 in appendix C. Regression 1 shows that richer households send away more migrants. The age of the household head or his/her spouse is negatively related to the number of migrants sent away. There seems to be a tendency of co-residence in old age. Household income and age cannot be used in the three-stage least squares regression as both variables are not exogenous to transfers and working hours. This leaves the number of migrants in the year 1993 as sole explanatory variable. Not surprisingly, the explanation power of the regression is driven by it. The R-squared remains at 60 percent. Regression 2 shows that only 4 percent of the variation of positive net transfers per capita can be explained when households receiving negative and zero net transfers are a assigned a zero for positive net transfers. Excluding these individuals, 28 percent of the variation is explained. Finally, regression (3) explains 6 percent of the variation in normal hours worked in the year 2000. Even the inclusion of normal hours worked in 1993 does not increase the explanation power. A Hausman test is performed to assess whether endogeneity is indeed problematic. It indicates that OLS would be inconsistent and that three-stage least squares is the correct and dominant estimation method.

Table 2.6: Three-Stage Least Squares Regression: Incentive effect on working hours of head/spouse

1999/2000	(1) Migrants	(2) Positive Net Transfers	(3) Normal Working Hours
Number of migrants		-.0125 (-0.48)	.2125** (1.98)
positive net transfers			-.6266** (-1.91)
non-labor income			-.0026 (-0.04)
asset value		-.1964*** (-4.20)	.1218 (0.60)
married		-1.756*** (-6.03)	-.0486 (-0.04)
not yet married			-7.987* (-1.82)
secondary education		-.7991*** (-3.84)	-.4962 (-0.65)
tertiary education		-.9643*** (-2.67)	-5.059*** (-3.72)
female			-1.479** (-2.08)
age			-.1828*** (-4.22)
ill			-3.273*** (-2.74)
poor today		.4725*** (3.03)	
insured		-.7037*** (-3.23)	
crisis 1998		.0622 (0.39)	
rural			-5.823*** (-8.74)
government worker			-4.956*** (-4.07)
private worker			2.234*** (2.88)
selfemployed with permanent workers			2.072 (0.98)
selfemployed with temporary workers			4.169*** (5.27)
household shocks:			
death of householder		.8070** (1.86)	
sickness of householder		.6963*** (2.46)	
crop loss		.4816* (1.65)	
natural disaster		.1099 (0.14)	
business or job loss		.5463 (1.06)	
decrease in income		.1863 (0.45)	
poor due to no opportunities			-.0093 (-0.01)
number of parents in the hh		-.4772** (-2.24)	
number of children in the hh		-.0661 (-1.31)	
characteristics of hh coresiding			
percentage primary education			-2.9998* (-1.74))
characteristics of hh non-coresiding			
percentage primary education		.6219* (1.86)	
percentage secondary education		1.655*** (3.81)	
percentage tertiary education		3.418*** (4.19)	
percentage out of province		.5674* (1.78)	
percentage disabled		-1.857 (-0.52)	
positive net transfers from siblings 1993		.5502*** (8.83)	
number of migrants 1993	.7473*** (89.01)		
Number of observations	5029	5029	5029
Source: Own calculations. T-statistic in parenthesis.			

Note: Province Dummies were also included in regression 3, but are not reported here. These provinces are North Sumatra, West Sumatra, South Sumatra, Lampung, West Java, Cental Java, Yogyakarta, East Java, Bali, West NusaTenggara, South Kalimantan and South Sulawesi. Left out province is Jakarta.

The results of the 3SLS approach[28] are presented in table 2.6.[29] In both regressions 1 and 2 one specific identifying variable is used. The instrument in regression 1 is the number of migrants in 1993. Positive net transfers from siblings of 1993 instrument for net transfers in 2000. Both instruments are not correlated with the residuals of the working hours regression.

Regression 1 finds that migrant networks exist over time and are associated with more migrants sent away in following years. Column 2 shows the regression explaining and instrumenting for positive net transfers. Net transfers take the value of zero if the de facto net amount received was negative or zero. The instrument "positive net transfers from siblings in 1993" identifies regression equation 2. The coefficient of the number of non-coresiding household members is negative, however not significant in explaining net transfers received.[30] However, the effect of educated migrants on net transfers is positive, sizable and significant.

Interestingly a household receives lower transfers if the members have access to other sources of insurance. Having experienced the crisis of 1998 negatively is not a reason for receiving more transfers. This is not surprising since the crisis has been a co-variate shock that hit almost all Indone-

[28] I have to strongly caution against overvaluing the results of this approach since it is hard to find good and also theoretical convincing instruments. The above mentioned first difference approach is clearly dominant.

[29] The graph B.6 in appendix B shows that residuals show no heteroscedastic pattern.

[30] The negative sign indicates that household members living outside the household tend to be potential petitioners instead of potential insurers. This result is in line with our short-run perspective and is indicated by the descriptive statistics presented above. Extensive panel data would be needed for a long-run perspective, where the potential insurance effect of non-coresiding household members should also be found.

sian households.[31] The subjective evaluation of a household's poverty is positively correlated with net remittances. The variable "poor" indicates whether a household assessed itself as poor or not. Several dummies for shocks possibly experienced by the household were included in the regression. If a household experienced the death or sickness of household members in the last years, it received significantly higher transfers. Furthermore a loss of crops though a drought or other event significantly drew more net remittances.[32] Therefore we can conclude that neediness is an important determinant of transfers. Transfers seem to insure the household, but do not automatically top up other insurance. On the other hand, having one's parents at home leads to significantly less transfers. Married individuals also get significantly lower transfers, as do well educated and wealthier individuals. The latter category of households is clearly less in need of transfers.

Additionally, the characteristics of migrants themselves are an important determinant of net transfers. Having more educated migrants outside the household increases the amount of transfers received. The higher the percentage of migrants living outside the province of the recipient the higher are positive net transfers received. Both variables determine the success of migrants. Living out of province ensures that migrants and the household of origin are less likely hit by the same covariate shocks and therefore facilitates mutual insurance.

31 The economic crisis took place in 1998. IFLS 3 data are not any more influenced by the crisis. It led to a drop of output by 15 percent in 1998 compared to the output level in 1997 and to inflation rates of 75-80 percent (Frankenberg et al., 1999).

32 The cost of shocks is not significantly positive related to positive net transfers. Households that experienced shocks rarely specified the cost of shocks. Therefore it is questionable whether it is an adequate measure.

Turning to regression 3, the negative and significant effect of positive net transfers per capita on working hours of the head and his/her spouse is in line with the predicted disincentive effects. This effect is mitigated partly by the positive effect of non-coresiding household members if the household receives positive net transfers. Thus couples have to work in order to provide transfers to potential petitioners. The direct effect of positive net transfers on working hours is given by a semi-elasticity of a -0.63 working hours decrease given a one percentage increase in positive net remittances. However, the combined effect of educated migrants on positive net remittances and working hours has to be calculated to evaluate the effective size of the disincentive effect. The combined effect - the semi-elasticity of an increase in the percentage of educated migrants on working hours - is calculated as follows:

$$
\begin{aligned}
W_i &= \alpha_i + \beta_1 \mathbf{X}_i + \beta_2 \mathbf{Xc} + \beta_3 V_i + \beta_4 T_i \\
&\quad + \beta_5 (P.M_{educated}^{-1} * M_{educated})_i \\
&\quad + \varepsilon_i \qquad (2.4) \\
T_i &= \alpha_i + \gamma_1 \mathbf{X}_i + \gamma_2 \mathbf{Xnc}_i + \gamma_3 \mathbf{S}_i + \gamma_4 P.M_{educated,i} \\
&\quad + \gamma_5 Z_i + \varepsilon_i \qquad (2.5) \\
\frac{\partial W}{\partial P.M_{educated}} * P.M_{educated} & \\
&= (-\beta_5 P.M_{educated}^{-2} * M_{educated} \\
&\quad + \beta_4 * (\gamma_4)) \\
&\quad * P.M_{educated} \qquad (2.6)
\end{aligned}
$$

To determine the size of the effect, the model is estimated using the combined average percentage of educated migrants (79 percent in 2000) as independent variable in regression 2.[33] A one percent increase in educated migrants leads to a 0.48 hours decrease in working hours. One more migrant educated would mean an 13 percent increase in the percentage of educated migrants. This leads to a approximate reduction in working hours of 6 hours. The effective disincentive is as well significant.

The finding of disincentive effects can be put into question if there exists an unobserved component that is negatively related to working hours and positively to net transfers. In the analysis we saw that the needy receive relatively more positive net transfers.[34] It might be the case that the households that receive high positive net transfers are further disadvantaged in finding a full-time or regular formal employment. These households will be employed in informal jobs. Evidence shows that the informal sector is often characterized by irregular and excessive of working hours (Musiolek, 2002; Fluitman and Momo, 2001; ILO, 2000). Looking at the analysed sample, average normal working hours in the formal sector (19,6 hours per week) are found to be slightly higher than normal working hours in the informal sector (18 hours per week). Moreover, a subjective variable measuring whether the majority of individuals in a village or town holds the opinion that the poor stay poor due to no opportunities to overcome poverty, is included in the regression. The

33 Coefficient of number of migrants β_5: 0.20 (5 percent significance level); coefficient of positive net transfers β_4: 0,70 (5 percent significance level); coefficient of percentage of educated migrants γ_4: 2,70 (1 percent significance level). The average number of educated migrants is 7.8.

34 The correlation between income per capita and positive net remittances per capita (concentrating on those households that receive amounts higher than zero) is positive but tiny (0.0003).

coefficient is negative but not significant in explaining the difference in normal working hours between individuals. Moreover, the province dummies included in the regression, left-out province being Jakarta, should capture regional disadvantages in finding a regular employment. Most of them are significantly negative meaning that in most provinces working hours are on average lower than in Jakarta.[35]

Normal hours of work are further explained using different employment categories. Excluded is the category of self-employed workers with no permanent or temporary workers. Private workers are those employed in the formal sector. This group and self-employed workers with temporary staff seem to work significantly more.

Moreover, a high non-labor income leads to less hours worked, but not significantly so. The wealth of the household has no influence. The marital status also seems to be unimportant in explaining normal hours worked per week. Married couples do not seem to work significantly less than divorced or widowed individuals. Not yet married individuals however do work less hours. Tertiary education leads to fewer hours worked. This may be a sign of more regular working hours. The higher the percentage of other co-residing household members with completed primary education the lower are hours worked. The negative coefficient might indicate that working hours of the head and spouse are lower because the co-residing members work also. The other variables show the expected signs. Females work significantly less hours than males. Living in rural areas means working fewer hours. This may also be related to fewer opportunities in the farm and non-farm sector of the economy. Being ill

[35] The province dummies were not reported in the appendix.

and older significantly reduces hours worked.

To conclude, the size of the disincentive effect suggested at the individual level is sizeable as well. However, the results of this section should not be overvalued as it has not been possible to find a strong instrument. The next section will therefore analyze the question of whether there are differing disincentive effects between sectors using the approach of section2.4.4.

2.4.5 Different Sectors

This section analyses whether there exist differences in behavioral effects of intra-family transfers between different sectors. So far the analysis has been ignoring that formal sector employees are less flexible in adjusting working hours.

The informal sector comprises self-employed persons working alone, with the help of temporary employers, or with no more than five permanent employers. Other definitions were tested without any difference in the empirical results. This definition is in line with the definitions and classifications provided in the United Nations System of National Accounts (Rev.4) and ILO informal sector surveys (ILO, 1999). When differentiating between the formal and informal sector, disincentive effects in the informal sector can be detected. Table 2.7 and 2.8 presents the results.[36] As expected, in the formal sector no clear evidence of a

[36] The results for the subsample of head and spouse using three-stage least squared are found in appendix C, tables B.6 and B.7. Note also that the regressions for the formal and agricultural sector using "first difference" are not reported in this study.

reduction in working hours due to a positive income shock in the past is found.

Table 2.7: First Differences - Normal Hours Worked per Week - Informal Sector

1993-2000	(1)	(2)	(3)	(4)
positive net transfers per capita	-2.158 (2.06)**			
Dummy for positive net tf		-6.618 (2.95)***		
positive gross transfers per capita			-1.874 (2.19)**	
net transfers per capita				-0.369 (3.00)***
rural	-12.896 (3.17)***	-18.548 (8.14)***	-17.261 (5.60)***	-18.483 (8.11)***
asset value per capita 1993	-0.405 (0.46)	-0.086 (0.17)	-0.217 (0.29)	-0.163 (0.32)
non-labor income per capita 1993	-0.609 (1.69)*	-0.247 (1.13)	-0.102 (0.36)	-0.291 (1.34)
age	-0.311 (2.09)**	-0.488 (5.09)***	-0.503 (4.15)***	-0.480 (4.99)***
female	-4.729 (0.92)	-5.668 (1.66)*	-5.112 (1.14)	-5.140 (1.50)
opportunities	6.793 (1.63)	8.756 (3.61)***	10.212 (3.14)***	8.616 (3.55)***
shock prior to 1993	-11.784 (1.60)	-9.830 (2.09)**	-10.004 (1.65)*	-9.992 (2.13)**
percentage primary education	44.073 (4.87)***	44.548 (8.28)***	41.942 (5.88)***	44.510 (8.28)***
percentage secondary education	60.238 (5.58)***	67.389 (10.21)***	63.680 (7.23)***	67.446 (10.22)***
percentage tertiary education	44.378 (0.81)	115.578 (4.84)***	136.043 (3.65)***	115.153 (4.82)***
normal working hours 1993	-0.680 (10.94)***	-0.658 (20.00)***	-0.661 (14.78)***	-0.659 (20.04)***
Constant	80.715 (4.80)***	69.225 (8.28)***	84.114 (6.18)***	67.531 (8.09)***
Observations	744	2463	1377	2463
R-squared	0.20	0.20	0.20	0.20

Source: Own calculations
T-statistic in parenthesis

Table 2.8: First Differences - Normal Hours Worked per Week - Formal Sector

1993-2000	(1)	(2)	(3)	(4)
positive net transfers per capita	-2.299 (1.77)*			
Dummy for positive net tf		-1.294 (0.48)		
positive gross transfers per capita			-3.955 (4.08)***	
net transfers per capita				0.004 (0.03)
rural	-5.824 (1.21)	-4.369 (1.73)*	-5.505 (1.59)	-4.478 (1.77)*
asset value per capita 1993	0.281 (0.28)	-1.205 (2.26)**	0.137 (0.17)	-1.183 (2.20)**
non-labor income per capita 1993	-0.071 (0.15)	-0.151 (0.63)	-0.052 (0.16)	-0.153 (0.64)
age	-0.335 (1.45)	-0.102 (0.74)	-0.285 (1.59)	-0.110 (0.80)
female	-9.331 (1.19)	-15.346 (3.03)***	-12.395 (1.90)*	-15.529 (3.06)***
opportunities	13.388 (2.38)**	10.423 (3.57)***	13.316 (3.17)***	10.379 (3.56)***
shock prior to 1993	-29.989 (1.76)*	-11.235 (1.16)	-12.038 (1.06)	-11.278 (1.17)
percentage primary education	42.220 (3.57)***	55.808 (8.48)***	48.310 (5.46)***	55.927 (8.50)***
percentage secondary education	52.723 (3.35)***	62.034 (7.42)***	57.729 (5.02)***	62.191 (7.44)***
percentage tertiary education	83.424 (1.35)	45.518 (1.61)	59.068 (1.49)	45.847 (1.62)
normal working hours 1993	-0.525 (6.71)***	-0.616 (16.25)***	-0.644 (12.18)***	-0.615 (16.22)***
Constant	65.588 (3.23)***	59.110 (6.42)***	85.761 (5.47)***	58.783 (6.40)***
Observations	457	1612	865	1612
R-squared	0.15	0.20	0.21	0.20

Source: Own calculations
T-statistic in parenthesis

Differentiating between the agricultural and non-agricultural sector[37] no clear evidence of a disincentive can be found. Results are presented in tables 2.9 and 2.10. One can argue that the Dummy variable for positive net remittances gives an unbiased estimate of the disincentive effect. The disincentive effect in the non-agricultural sector is higher than the one in the agricultural sector. Furthermore, in appendix B results are shown when using the three-stage least squares method on the individual-level sample of head and spouse of the household. Here, a disincentive effect can only be detected in the non-agricultural sector.

[37] Individuals were asked specifically in which sector of the economy they are working.

Table 2.9: First Differences - Normal Hours Worked per Week - Non-agricultural Sector

1993-2000	(1)	(2)	(3)	(4)
positive net transfers per capita	-1.545 (0.91)			
Dummy for positive net tf		-6.997 (1.91)*		
positive gross transfers per capita			-1.923 (1.53)	
net transfers per capita				-0.278 (1.50)
asset value per capita 1993	0.156 (0.12)	-1.062 (1.41)	-0.446 (0.42)	-1.081 (1.42)
non-labor income per capita 1993	-1.386 (2.28)**	-0.601 (1.92)*	-0.908 (2.08)**	-0.620 (1.98)**
age	-0.222 (0.76)	-0.142 (0.80)	-0.082 (0.36)	-0.151 (0.85)
female	-4.485 (0.54)	-8.915 (1.69)*	-13.162 (1.95)*	-8.804 (1.66)*
opportunities	20.966 (2.88)***	15.678 (3.99)***	18.445 (3.32)***	15.608 (3.97)***
shock prior to 1993	-0.655 (0.04)	1.399 (0.12)	2.887 (0.23)	0.835 (0.07)
percentage primary education	45.888 (2.83)***	38.748 (4.20)***	32.658 (2.64)***	39.063 (4.23)***
percentage secondary education	43.318 (2.53)**	58.957 (6.23)***	47.107 (3.62)***	59.139 (6.24)***
percentage tertiary education	204.823 (3.16)***	97.557 (3.68)***	120.788 (3.13)***	98.369 (3.71)***
normal working hours 1993	-0.450 (4.71)***	-0.618 (12.37)***	-0.605 (8.74)***	-0.619 (12.39)***
Constant	42.995 (1.53)	58.479 (4.32)***	62.878 (2.94)***	56.515 (4.19)***
Observations	324	1160	616	1160
R-squared	0.16	0.17	0.17	0.17

Source: Own calculations
T-statistic in parenthesis

Table 2.10: First Differences - Normal Hours Worked per Week - Agricultural Sector

1993-2000	(1)	(2)	(3)	(4)
positive net transfers per capita	-1.044 (0.73)			
Dummy for positive net tf		-5.885 (1.87)*		
positive gross transfers per capita			-1.703 (1.40)	
net transfers per capita				-0.321 (1.80)*
asset value per capita 1993	-1.386 (1.08)	-0.812 (0.97)	-0.134 (0.12)	-0.890 (1.06)
non-labor income per capita 1993	-0.166 (0.33)	-0.417 (1.24)	0.024 (0.06)	-0.451 (1.35)
age	-0.375 (1.69)*	-0.515 (3.49)***	-0.576 (3.28)***	-0.511 (3.46)***
female	-6.743 (0.85)	-10.660 (1.85)*	-6.850 (0.95)	-10.119 (1.74)*
opportunities	9.438 (1.75)*	8.771 (2.57)**	9.465 (2.22)**	8.575 (2.52)**
shock prior to 1993	-13.028 (1.63)	-13.237 (2.32)**	-15.078 (2.17)**	-13.445 (2.36)**
percentage primary education	18.666 (1.46)	34.554 (4.07)***	23.130 (2.27)**	34.671 (4.09)***
percentage secondary education	29.360 (1.94)*	48.158 (4.93)***	39.345 (3.31)***	48.456 (4.97)***
percentage tertiary education	-35.387 (0.53)	120.486 (3.38)***	71.748 (1.29)	121.140 (3.40)***
normal working hours 1993	-0.554 (6.37)***	-0.598 (12.20)***	-0.579 (9.06)***	-0.599 (12.20)***
Constant	69.260 (3.01)***	61.119 (4.46)***	67.089 (3.52)***	59.877 (4.37)***
Observations	335	1008	586	1008
R-squared	0.16	0.17	0.17	0.17
Source: Own calculations				
T-statistic in parenthesis				

Note: Including the number of missing household members did not change regression outcomes.

It can therefore be concluded that there indeed seem to exist disincentive effects for individuals of working-age. It is important to distinguish between sectors to detect the true behavioral effect of intra-family transfers.

2.5 Conclusion and Outlook

The empirical results can be interpreted twofold. At first sight, the concerns of some development practitioners seem to be validated to some extent.

At the household level, the disincentive is significant meaning that resources are used to support other household members and these reduce effort.[38] The results for different sectors show that individuals of working age indeed react to the incentive to lower effort.[39]

There are potential positive effects of remittances. A household can use remittances to smooth household income. The empirical analysis found evidence for the insuring character of remittances. Therefore households might simply be in the position to substitute uncertain income earned in the informal sector with a more reliable income source. Additionally, households might substitute income earned under poor working conditions using remittances.

The household data of 2000 and 1993 from Indonesia give a picture

38 As long as child work, for example, is reduced through transfers, transfers are welfare enhancing and have no economically negative effect. Even if adult children living in the household significantly reduce working hours to spend more time in school or vocational education this would be deemed an economically desirable effect.

39 There might also exist an effect on household composition, which has not been analyzed here.

of net providers of transfers and not so much net recipients. Household members, especially those migrating within their own country, are potential petitioners and not only insurers of their close relatives. Intra-family transfers in Indonesia form part of a mutual insurance system. The fact of being a potential petitioner and a potential insurer simultaneously leads to a compensation for the disincentive effects of transfers.

The analysis shows also that migration is an effective diversifying strategy for a household only if the migrants are educated. The fact that migration may not be crowned with success especially for the poor and uneducated is not new. Most of them end up in no better situation.

Furthermore, the empirical results may imply that international remittances may cause even more severe disincentive effects. First, this is for the reason of missing mutuality. Second, the moral hazard problem is more pronounced. Furthermore, the analysis shows that richer households send more migrants. Only these can afford the high cost of migration. The cost of migrating abroad is even higher. This makes it unlikely that a significant amount of poor households working in subsistence agriculture can afford migration as a diversifying strategy. In this case, there could exist positive incentive effects.

Although comprehensive, this analysis misses some important aspects. Due to data shortages it was not possible to introduce a monetary measure of the disincentive. This would be necessary to quantify the amount of income that is lost and calculate whether the net effect on income is still positive.

Furthermore it would be interesting to be able to assess whether children spend more time in school if the household regularly receives remittances. Therefore time-use statistics would be needed to investigate other possible welfare-enhancing effects of remittances at the household level.

Chapter 3

Income Diversification and Poverty in a Growing Agricultural Economy: The Case of Ghana

3.1 Introduction

It is well established that rural households in Sub-Saharan Africa derive their incomes from a variety of sources, in particular from local non-farm activities and remittances from former household members. Although many observers seem to agree on an increased role for such activities outside agriculture, there is not much empirical work on change in patterns of rural income diversification, i.e. structural change, and its driving forces.

This chapter is based on joint work with Jann Lay.

For an analysis of change it may prove useful to depart from the observation that rural households diversify out of agriculture because of different motivations. On the one hand, poor rural households may hence embrace multiple livelihoods primarily to ensure survival, as they are forced to diversify mainly because they lack sufficient agricultural assets to sustain subsistence (Reardon and Taylor, 1996; Haggblade et al., 2005). On the other hand, richer rural households with higher asset endowments will choose to diversify their livelihoods to maximise returns to their assets. Such activities typically exhibit entry barriers that the poor are not able to overcome. This dichotomy of diversification illustrates the strong link to welfare outcomes. Finally, households insure themselves against harvest shortfalls through engagement in activities outside crop farming (Reardon et al. 1992).

Such a dichotomy of diversification strategies implies that the stylized fact of increasingly diversified livelihoods in rural Sub-Saharan Africa can either be explained by increased desperation, as suggested by Bryceson (2002a), by better economic opportunities outside agriculture in a growing economy, or even both. From this perspective, this paper examines the patterns of income diversification for the case of rural Ghana during the 1990s, a period of sustained growth in the country. More specifically, we analyse the underlying motivations for diversification as well as related changes in inequality and poverty using the country-wide Living Standards Measurement Surveys of 1991 and 1998. To our knowledge, all existing studies on the topic from the Sub-Saharan context rely on one cross-section or on short-term panels. We use the two cross-sections for a detailed descriptive analysis of changes in diversification behaviour, which is then complemented by the estimation of a multivariate choice model on the pooled cross-sections. Finally, we perform disaggregated incidence analyses to assess the relationship between those changes in diversification behaviour and welfare outcomes.

The paper finds that rural households in Ghana indeed increasingly diversify their livelihoods by both increased migration and more local non-farm employment. Yet, only asset-rich households seem to be successful diversifiers. Poorer households increase the income share in particular from local non-farm activities through more participation while returns to diversifying activities stagnate or even decrease. In this sense, diversification appears to be driven to a large extent by desperation and asset-poor households increasingly diversify and remain poor.

The paper is structured as follows. We first review the literature on rural income diversification and its welfare implications. Then we present our empirical results. A final section concludes.

3.2 Income Diversification, Poverty, and Inequality

The contribution of non-agricultural activities to household income in the developing world in general and sub-Saharan Africa in particular is substantial. Haggblade et al. (2005) observe that local non-farm income contributes between 30 to 45 percent of rural household incomes in the developing world. Reardon et al. (1998) put this share at 42 percent for sub-Saharan Africa, while Reardon (1999) gives estimates of 32 percent and 40 percent for Asia and Latin America, respectively. Ellis (2000) reports somewhat higher figures from case studies in sub-Saharan Africa in a range of 30 to 50 percent. Local non-farm activities are often pursued through self-employment, but there is also a non-agricultural wage labour market, although this market is typically small in the rural sub-Saharan African context. Significant amounts of money and in-kind transfers are remitted by international and internal migrants. International remittance flows to developing countries made up 221.3 billion USD in 2006 (World Bank, 2006 (1)). The figure for Ghana indicates an inflow of 105 million USD in 2006 (World Bank (1), 2007). Internal remittances also constitute a big share of household income. Cox and Jimenez (1990) review studies on private intra-family transfers in developing countries. They find that 20-90 percent of households in developing countries receive private transfers, comprising 2-20 percent of household income. In the same time frame only 15 percent of households in the United States received such transfers, comprising only 1 percent of household income on average.

In order to analyse the patterns of income diversification and the link to welfare outcomes, it is useful to distinguish survival-led and opportunity-led diversification. When diversification is pursued to ensure survival, for example because of declining opportunities in agriculture possibly related to population pressure and land fragmentation, or natural disasters, such as droughts, it is also referred to as distress-push diversification (e.g. Islam, 1997; Reardon et al., 2000; Barrett, Reardon and Webb, 2001). Such diversification will be in low-return non-agricultural activities and may be an indication that the non-agricultural sector - both local and elsewhere - is absorbing labour that cannot be employed in agriculture. In contrast, rural households may face new opportunities outside agriculture because of increasing local demand for non-agricultural goods and services. Migrants may find employment in urban regions or better opportunities in agriculture in other rural regions. If non-agricultural income diversification can be traced back to such factors, it is also regarded as demand-pull.[1]

Furthermore, non-agricultural diversification constitutes an important means to deal with risk and smooth income and consumption in rural areas. This is not surprising since agricultural livelihoods are often subject to great uncertainty. In such an environment, diversification aims at lower covariate risk between different household activities to smooth consumption (Bryceson, 1999; Dercon, 1998 and 2002; Francis and Hoddinott, 1993)[2]. While rural household risk can be reduced by venturing into non-agricultural activities, risk considerations may also play a role when deciding between different types of non-agricultural activities. If high-return non-farm activities are more risky than low-return activities, households that are able to overcome possible entry barriers may engage in both types of non-agricultural activities according to their risk

1 Demand-pull diversification does not necessarily have to be high-return diversification, as, for example, a migrant can be "pulled" to urban areas without finding high-return employment.

2 It is useful to distinguish between ex-ante risk management and ex-post risk coping strategies. Engagement in high-return non-agricultural activities represents an ex-ante risk management strategy, as it is unlikely that entry barriers can be easily overcome after a negative shock. In contrast, low-return non-agricultural diversification will figure prominently as an ex-post coping strategy, i.e. households will relocate labour towards these activities after they have been hit by a negative agricultural shock, typically a weather shock. Yet, in particular poorer household may also be willing to accept lower returns than in agriculture ex-ante in exchange for lower covariate risk.

preferences. Yet, migration may be the most adequate strategy to lower covariate risk, as shocks experienced by migrants and the household of origin are less likely to be correlated. Migration serves as a mutual insurance mechanism. This explains why net transfer flows to households might be even negative. Several studies on migration and remittances (Boayke-Yiadom and McKay, 2007; Schueler, 2007) indeed find that migrants are costly.

Migration and non-farm participation are driven by a similar calculus of the household. On both strategies there is a large empirical literature that often treats them separately. Empirical contributions on participation in non-farm employment and migration tend to stress the influence of household characteristics on diversification decisions. Asset availability as well as educational and skill endowments have been highlighted as key participation determinants of non-farm diversification and high-return activities, in particular (Ferreira and Lanjouw, 2001; Lanjouw, 2001; Barrett, Reardon and Webb, 2001; Escobal, 2001; Dercon and Krishnan, 1996; Reardon, 1997). Whereas entry barriers to engage in low-return non-farm activities should be low, they can be considerable for those yielding higher returns. In the presence of underdeveloped credit markets, high-return non-farm activities typically require sufficient cash income, in particular from livestock, cash cropping, and/or remittances, both for initial investment and as working capital (Reardon et al., 2000; Barrett, Bezuneh and Aboud, 2000). Similarly, initial asset endowments play an important role, in particular land (e.g. Seppala, 1996; Elbers and Lanjouw, 2001; Marenya et al., 2003). For instance, Elbers and Lanjouw (2001) show that land scarcity is related to participation in a low-return non-agricultural activity while more landholdings seem to provide collateral for investment in high-return non-agricultural businesses. Another household level factor correlated with participation in non-agricultural activities is the size and structure of the household (Corral and Reardon, 2001; Reardon, 1997). Reardon (1997) shows that a larger size enables households to supply more labour to non-agricultural activities, since sufficient family members remain at home to meet labour demands for agricultural subsistence. As regards community level determinants, most empirical studies confirm an important role for physical and institutional infrastructure, such as paved roads, efficient communication facilities and provision of rural electrification.

With regard to migration it is helpful to distinguish different kinds of migration. Overall, the kind of migration observed the most is migration of a part of household members and not the household as a whole. Furthermore, migration may be seasonal, circular, rural-urban or international. International migration exhibits the highest entry constraints. Migration networks within home countries and in host countries reduce these entry constraints to migration significantly. Decisions on the migration of household members are also found to be affected importantly by educational and asset characteristics of households (Greenwood, 1997; Lucas, 1997; Deshingkar and Grimm, 2004). A key constraint to migration is the availability of labour within the household. Deshingkar and Start (2003) find that labour-scarce households do not migrate. The poorest households usually cannot migrate due to labour scarcity and resource requirements (Deshingkar and Grimm, 2004).

All these conditions that constrain or enable households to diversify are subject to change. Rapid population growth and shortages of fertile land are often identified as the major cause for the rise of non-farm activities and migration in Sub-Saharan Africa (Bryceson and Jamal 1997, Barrett et al. 2000, Bryceson 2002b). In contrast, other factors at the household-level, in particular the expansion of education may enable quite a few households to overcome skill barriers and earn higher returns from local non-farm activities or migration. Yet, it may also be that an increased supply of (relatively) skilled labour depresses the returns to those activities. In addition, technological advances, better infrastructure, the intensification of links with markets outside the local economy, local engines of growth, such as commercial agriculture or proximity to an urban area, or simply per capita income growth and increased demand for non-food goods and services can lead to a growing non-farm sector (Reardon 1999, Haggblade et al. 2002). Furthermore, the structural reform programs that many African countries have undergone in the late 1980s and early 1990s have certainly shaped the patterns of growth and household portfolios in these countries since then. Possibly, reforms had their most pronounced impact on income portfolios through altering the returns in agricultural activities, for example in cash crop sectors, which often had been subject to heavy regulation. Furthermore, macroeconomic stability that has been recorded by most reform countries since the mid-1990s may have strengthened farmers' trust into markets thereby contributing to increased market participation and specialization. On the other hand, it is not clear whether agriculture, or at least certain sub-sectors, have been able to compete in liberalized markets where prices are determined internationally. Overall, these changes in the conditions or drivers of diversification have been subject to relatively little empirical scrutiny. Often, the view on diversification being mainly desperation-led is at best backed by a snapshot of household diversification behaviour, i.e. most studies take a static view when interpreting the findings on the structure of non-farm sector participation or migration.

Changes in income portfolios will also have important welfare and distributional implications. All in all, there seems to be a positive correlation between wealth and diversification in rural Africa (Barrett et al. 2001). If diversifying incomes go mainly to the better-off, as for instance local non-farm income often does, growth of this sector is inequality increasing (Elbers and Lanjouw 2001). However, others find that non-farm income is concentrated among the poor, so that an increase in these incomes is eventually pro-poor (van der Berg and Kumbi 2006, Adams 2002). These seemingly contradictory findings can possibly be reconciled by taking into account the distinct motivations underlying diversification. For example, if the non-farm sector can be characterized largely by low-return and desperation-led activities, we would expect a pro-poor effect of non-farm income growth. Accordingly, Lay et al. (2007) find the expansion of opportunity-led local non-farm employment to have little impact on poverty, while growth of income from the desperation-led activities significantly reduces poverty. In such a case, the overall impact of diversification on the income distribution remains mixed.

Again, the above empirical work typically builds on cross-sectional data, which implies that poverty and distributional implications are evaluated at the margin. At the margin means that income from a particular source is "simulated" to increase by a marginal amount (e.g. Reardon et al., 1992; Lay et al., 2007). Although useful for illustrative purposes, such simulations can also be misleading, since they do not allow for behavioural response that can have important distributional implications. If for example income from opportunity-led high-return non-farm employment rises, it may well be that this increase enables some households to jump over entry hurdles. The welfare effect of this discrete change in behaviour of some households will of course be different from the effect of a uniform increase in high-return income for those already engaged in this sector.

The behavioural responses to remittances and the corresponding welfare effect are even more complex. Firstly, remittances are transfers of family-members who cannot perfectly observe other household members' behaviour any more. Due to this informational asymmetry remittances might cause a negative incentive effect on work effort (Rozelle, 1999; Azam and Gubert, 2002; Andersen and Terjerina, 2005; Schueler, 2007). Secondly, migrants might be hard to substitute if labour markets work imperfectly in rural areas, therefore restricting household farm income and production (Rozelle et al. 1999). While the latter effects of remittances would be welfare-decreasing, remittances could also be used for investment in agriculture (Azam and Gubert, 2002)[3] and could effectively insure the household. Woodruff (2001) finds that households with an association to migrant networks have a higher probability to be the owner of a micro-enterprise. This could be due to returning migrants that in-

[3] Azam and Gubert (2005) examine both the disincentive and accumulation effect of remittances. They find remittances to reduce agricultural productivity through moral hazard even though more productive assets are used by the household. However, they do not consider the additional effect of foregone labour in their analysis.

vest their savings or remittances. The net effect of foregone labour and remittances has been found to be negative for rural households (Rozelle et al. 1999).

Local non-farm income is often reinvested in improved agricultural technology. Empirical evidence shows that non-farm income is indeed the main source of investment for raising farm productivity (Reardon et al., 1994; Reardon, 1997, 1998; Abdulai and Huffman, 2000; Ellis and Freeman, 2004).

The recent literature on rural livelihoods has stressed that these mechanisms can give rise to vicious and virtuous cycles (Ellis and Freeman, 2004). In vicious cycles low asset endowments and low asset productivity force poor rural households into desperation-led diversification, which in turn reduces agricultural productivity. Such poverty traps are eventually caused by entry barriers that prevent households from gradually shifting from lower return to higher return activities (Barrett 2004; Abdulai and Huffman 2005). This outcome is particularly likely in case of very low asset endowments combined with severe financial market failures, but can also result from poor climatic conditions, poor infrastructure, missing markets for agricultural products, and under-developed linkages between agriculture and the rest of the economy.

We are of the opinion that the concepts of the literature on rural livelihoods are probably more useful in examining structural change at the macro level than conventional notions of sectors (modern vs. traditional, formal vs. informal). National account statistics can give an overview of the importance of certain sectors in the economy. They cannot inform about shifts in sectoral labour participation at the household level.

Whether the growing Ghanaian economy has seen more desperation- or opportunity-led diversification will hence be a core question of the subsequent empirical analyses.

3.3 The Ghanaian Case: Patterns and Changes

Today Ghana is considered an African success story (Bogetic et al., 2007; Coulombe and Wodon, 2007; IMF, 2007; IMF, 2000). Since 1983 average growth of 4.6 percent was considerably higher than in other sub-Saharan economies. In contrast, at the beginning of the 1980s Ghana was battered by fiscal imbalances, deteriorating terms of trade and political unrest. A period of market orientation followed the coup of Rawlings that was interrupted by the implementation of a new constitution that paved the way for the first democratic election in 1992. This however led to a power struggle and political unrest, fiscal imbalances, as well as high inflation rates were a consequence. A few years later Ghana was back on the track of market orientation and macroeconomic as well as political stability.

Ghana's economy is dominated by agriculture that accounts for 40 percent of GDP (Bogetic et al., 2007; IMF, 2000). Growth in agriculture is seen as the key determinant of the substantial reduction in poverty achieved in the 1990s (World Bank (2), 2007). While yields improved only slightly, agricultural growth mainly stems from area expansion. Slow agricultural growth has been attributed to a lack of improvement in the productivity of main food crops, missing support for innovation in small-scale agriculture as well as poor transport and distribution channels (Aryeetey, 2005). Moreover, the parastatal monopoly in cocoa marketing has not been eliminated (World Bank, 1995; IMF, 2000) although reforms ensured that cocoa farmers receive a higher share of world market prices (Kanbur, 1994).[4]

National accounts data suggest that, in the 1990s, the services were the fastest growing sector of the economy, driven by growth of "wholesale, retail, restaurants and hotels" as well as "transport, storage and communications". Industrial growth was driven by the subsectors "energy and construction". Taking into account population growth, this development led to an increase in employment opportunities only in urban areas, especially Accra (Bogetic et al., 2007). Yet overall, World Bank and IMF highlight that the Ghanaian economy seems to exhibit negligible signs of a structural transformation in the 1990s, in particular in terms of the sectoral composition of the economy (IMF, 2000; Bogetic et al., 2007; McKay and Aryeetey 2007; World Bank, 2007).

In this regard, the important social and economic reforms and public investments that have been undertaken by the Ghanaian authorities appear to have had little effect. One of the most important reform programs was the one aimed at reforming the education system of Ghana. This reform process started in 1987 and resulted in the so-called "Free Compulsory Universal Basic Education" (FCUBE) strategy of the government in 1996 (Akyeampong, 2004). The FCUBE had the target to put into practice free primary education for every child in Ghana until 2005. A World Bank evaluation found evidence that reforms were successful in increasing enrollment, improving test scores and reducing illiteracy

[4] More recently smallholder cocoa farming experienced a boom through the use of new technologies and higher world market prices even though a low price transmission to farmers was found in general (World Bank (2), 2007.

rates, even though absolute levels of student achievement are still low (World Bank, 2004). Public investment was not limited to the education sector: Economic infrastructure recovered through massive public investments following the economic upswing in 1991 that led to government revenue excluding foreign aid of 15 percent of GDP. Investments comprised improvement of roads, electricity and water supply and better telephone communication (Kanbur, 1994). Corruption has been found to be prevalent in public and private sectors. 86 percent of the households interviewed in the Ghana Governance and Corruption Survey of 2000 see corruption as a major problem in the public sector (World Bank, 2000). It is therefore not surprising that visible success of the mentioned intended investments in infrastructure has been minor.

Another significant change in the Ghanaian economy is the massive increase in private capital flows from abroad. These rose steadily up to 105 million US Dollars in 2006 (World Bank (1), 2007).

Most reports suggest that the Ghanaian economy has not seen major transformations, at least in rural areas. Yet, as the following anlyses show, a look at the patterns of change in rural income portfolios and the underlying determinants yields a different picture. The subsequent analysis focuses on rural areas that still account for 66.8 percent of Ghana's population in 1991 (66.3 percent in 1998) and host the majority of the country's poor.

3.4 Increasing Diversification: Descriptive Analysis

Overall, income diversification increases significantly in the 1990s. As illustrated in table 3.1, the percentage of diversifying farm households with at least one source of non-farm income increased from 76 to 85 percent between 1991 and 1998. Diversification is defined as participation in the local non-farm sector through wage- or self-employment and participation in migration. A household participates in migration if some household members migrated to villages different from the household's village of residence. These migrants might be temporary or permanent migrants. Migration is slightly more important than local non-farm employment as diversification strategy and this does not change much. Most households in fact engage in both diversification strategies at once, followed by farming households sending away migrants only and participating in the non-farm sector only. The overall increase between 1991 and 1998 is entirely due to more households pursuing both strategies rather than a single one.

Table 3.1: Participation rates by households characteristics, 1991 and 1998.

	perc. of hh 1991	perc. of hh 1998	Diversifying 1991	Diversifying 1998	With Migrants 1991	With Migrants 1998	Non-farm sector 1991	Non-farm sector 1998	Both strategies 1991	Both strategies 1998
Regions										
All			76,3	84,9	55,0	64,0	50,0	60,3	28,8	39,4
Western	11,4	15,0	70,5	88,2	53,5	69,2	43,6	61,1	26,6	42,1
Central	13,5	12,8	79,6	91,0	55,6	68,1	57,0	70,9	33,1	48,0
Volta	1,8	0,9	73,7	88,0	34,2	79,7	52,6	64,7	13,2	56,4
Greater A	19,0	13,6	81,0	86,8	59,6	60,5	55,6	69,9	34,2	43,6
Eastern	11,9	16,5	82,4	88,7	58,0	69,2	55,2	63,9	30,8	44,5
Ashanti	18,9	14,6	79,7	86,7	63,2	70,6	49,6	57,7	33,1	41,6
Brong Ahafo	14,2	13,4	76,6	76,8	58,9	55,0	42,8	46,9	25,1	25,1
Northern	9,3	13,2	54,1	74,5	24,0	52,1	41,3	50,6	11,2	28,3
Age of hh head										
-25	6,5	3,8	45,6	76,3	50,0	55,3	45,6	44,9	23,5	23,8
25-35	23,4	20,5	54,7	86,2	50,2	62,3	54,7	64,1	29,2	40,2
35-55	41,8	48,2	54,4	86,7	57,0	63,7	54,4	66,9	32,3	44,0
55-	28,4	27,5	40,8	82,1	57,0	67,0	40,8	47,8	24,4	32,8
Sex of hh head										
male	72,7	71,5	75,3	84,8	53,2	63,7	50,3	61,8	28,2	40,7
female	27,3	28,5	78,8	85,1	59,7	64,7	49,3	56,5	30,2	36,2
Highest level of education completed of hh head										
none	65,2	48,3	73,4	80,9	52,6	62,0	45,9	51,9	25,1	33,0
primary	4,2	12,4	74,2	88,3	62,9	63,3	46,1	60,1	34,8	35,2
secondary	28,9	35,1	81,6	87,9	58,0	66,2	57,2	68,2	33,6	46,5
higher	1,7	4,2	100,0	95,2	74,3	70,4	97,1	90,5	71,4	65,8
Land size (acres)										
0 - 1	50,3	46,2	80,5	86,4	54,0	61,5	58,4	67,6	31,9	42,8
1 - 2	23,1	23,0	71,7	88,0	54,0	67,7	44,4	60,3	26,7	40,1
2 - 4	15,7	17,2	72,1	81,1	56,4	64,4	41,5	52,1	25,8	35,4
4 -	11,0	13,6	72,7	79,4	59,7	65,7	35,9	45,5	22,9	31,8
Source: Own Calculations.										

Table 3.2 shows the income shares that rural households derive from the respective activities. Though income data is measured with difficulty in household suveys, the data is deemed to be a good approximation of the importance of different income sources.[5] The average share of non-farm income amounts to 38.4 percent in 1991 and remains unchanged until 1998. The (household income) weighted non-farm share stands at almost 50 percent in 1991 and in fact falls afterwards. This indicates that poorer households derive a higher share of income from the non-farm sector in 1998. The increase in non-farm participation combined with a constant (or even falling weighted) income share may be taken as a first indication of a stagnant non-farm economy that grows in employment terms because of the lack of alternatives.

Remittances account for a relatively small portion of household income. Weighted, they make up only 2 percent of total income earned by rural households in 1991. By 1998, this percentage share has increased to almost 3 percent. Yet, the average share has climbed to almost 7 percent in 1998, indicating that poorer households rely more heavily on remittances.

5 It might be difficult for the household to remember the exact level of income, but judging the importance of different income sources should be easier.

Table 3.2: Income shares of from different activities, by household characteristics, 1991 and 1998.

	Share of income from					
	Non-farm		Remittances		Farm	
	1991	1998	1991	1998	1991	1998
All	38,4	38,5	4,5	6,9	57,1	54,6
All (weighted)	49,3	46,4	2,0	2,8	48,7	50,8
Age of hh head						
-25	35,2	32,3	4,7	6,5	60,1	61,1
25-35	42,3	45,9	3,1	4,6	54,5	49,6
35-55	41,8	46,8	3,5	4,0	54,6	49,2
55-	31,0	30,5	6,8	11,1	62,2	58,4
Sex of hh head						
male	38,2	42,2	2,0	3,3	59,8	54,4
female	39,0	40,1	11,2	13,2	49,8	46,7
Highest level of education completed of hh head						
none	34,7	35,6	5,4	7,8	59,9	56,5
primary	35,2	40,1	5,8	6,2	59,0	53,7
secondary	44,7	46,9	2,3	4,1	53,0	49,0
higher	83,7	70,3	0,3	3,9	16,0	25,8
Land size (acres)						
0 - 1	47,2	50,7	5,2	6,4	47,6	42,9
1 - 2	32,5	40,1	4,5	5,9	63,0	54,0
2 - 4	29,3	31,1	3,2	5,4	67,4	63,5
4 -	23,7	26,5	2,7	6,5	73,6	67,0
Source: Own Calculations.						

The regions of Ghana exhibit considerable socio-economic differences and this also holds to some extent for diversification strategies. Between the Ghanaian regions the share of diversifying households fluctuates between 70 and 85 percent in 1991 with the exception of the Northern Region. The diversifying share appears to converge to about 85 to 90 percent in 1998 in all provinces except Brong Ahafo and the Northern Region. The diversification patterns in those two regions are hence particularly noteworthy. Examining the two diversification strategies separately, developments seem to be fairly similar across the regions, again with the same exceptions.

The Northern Region is the province where households diversified least in both years. Yet, still more than half of the rural households are diversified in 1991 and the increase of more than 20 percentage points is the strongest of all regions. Most of this increase is driven by migration. Surveys analysing migration patterns in Ghana, find that the Brong Ahafo and part of the Ashanti region in the middle of Ghana, one of the leading producers of grain, cereals and tubers, attract mainly farm migrants from the North (Codjoe, 2006). There is evidence that these migrants have more farmed land, earn more farm income and use more mechanized farming practices than local farmers (Codjoe, 2006). This indicates that a major part of migration from the Northern Region is driven by the pull factor of better opportunities in agriculture in the so-called transitional agro-ecological zone. Brong Ahafo's agricultural potential and the fact that it receives migrants rather than sending them away might also explain why the share of diversifying households in this region stays constant and why the share of households with migrants even declines. This may also hold for the Ashanti region to some extend.

Diversification increases with the age of the household head, but declines after the age of 55. This decline in diversification is driven by a sharp decline in non-farm sector participation in old-age. Migration increases with age, as does the average income share, which can be partly explained by migrants that serve as supporters in old-age[6]. Over time both migration and non-farm participation increase with no particular pattern.

The gap between male and female-headed households' involvement in activities outside agriculture appears to be relatively small. Yet, when interpreting these figures it needs to be taken into account that many households are female-headed just because husbands are seasonal or long-term migrants. This is reflected in the much higher reliance on remittances of those households. The relatively small difference in terms of migration may suggest that other female-headed households (e.g. widowed or divorced) are less prone (or able) to send household members away. Non-farm involvement in 1991 is similar for male and female-headed households, as is engagement in both strategies. Yet, between 1991 and 1998 non-farm participation increases considerably more among male-headed households.

When households are disaggregated by educational achievement of the household head an interesting pattern emerges over time. The educational composition of rural households (measured by the head's education) changes considerably in the 1990s possibly reflecting the outcomes

[6] The fact that a household is more likely to participate in migration the older the household head is also likely to reflect the preference of younger household members to leave the agricultural sector or the region.

of the educational reforms outlined above. Diversification increases for all educational groups except for the best educated. Participation in local non-farm activities grows particularly strongly for household whose head has primary or secondary education. Nevertheless households whose head has higher than secondary education (about 5 percent of rural households in 1998) are still more often found to diversify. In the 1990s, these households appear to specialise in agriculture; participation in and income from the local non-farm sector declines considerably. Another notable finding is that all other households' income share from local non-farm income increases only slightly despite much higher rates in participation.

As expected diversification rates are higher for land-poor households with less than one acre of arable land - who account for almost half of the rural population. Yet, between 1991 and 1998 households with 1-2 acres reach a similar (even slightly higher) degree of diversification. Strategies of land-poor and land-rich farmers differ. Non-farm participation rates tend to decrease with land size in both years and all groups increasingly engage in the non-farm economy. In contrast, while more land makes households more likely to have migrants in 1991, this relationship seems to break down in 1998 and migration becomes a strategy particularly strongly pursued by households with 1-2 acres. It should be noted that the increase in migration participation of this group goes along with a relatively modest rise in the remittance income share.

Most of the above household characteristics are important determinants of a households' income earning capacity. However, the observations about diversification patterns would make it difficult to a priori judge how the relationship between income and diversification would look like. Overall, we find a positive correlation between income and diversification for both years (table 3.3) and for all income groups does diversification increase considerably in the 1990s. This holds for both local non-farm employment and migration. Only with regard to pursuing both strategies at once the "diversification gap" between poor and rich households widens. In 1998, more than half of the households in the richest income quintile have migrants and pursue a non-farm activity.

More pronounced are the differences in changes in income shares between 1991 and 1998. As table 3.4 illustrates, the share of income derived from farming activities declines for all income quintiles, except for the richest. This decline is most pronounced for the poorest quintile that substitutes farm especially through local non-farm income. Poorer households rely more heavily on remittance income - despite lower participation rates. This holds even more strongly in 1998 than in 1991.

Table 3.3: Participation by income quintiles, 1991 and 1998.

	perc. of hh		Diversifying		With Migrants		Non-farm sector		Both strategies	
	1991	1998	1991	1998	1991	1998	1991	1998	1991	1998
Income Quintile										
1	20.0	20.0	60,6	69,6	47,6	54,1	23,0	33,1	10,0	17,6
2	20.0	20.0	73,8	81,1	53,3	58,7	43,7	52,1	23,2	29,7
3	20.0	20.0	79,3	87,4	53,6	66,2	57,5	65,1	31,8	43,9
4	20.0	20.0	82,9	92,2	60,0	67,5	59,7	72,1	36,8	47,4
5	20.0	20.0	83,6	90,1	60,0	70,8	64,3	71,5	40,7	52,3
Source: Own Calculations.										

In general, income shares of non-agricultural sources increase relatively little despite considerably higher participation rates. In the following, we therefore analyze in more detail the "intensity" of diversification by looking at the number of household members involved in diversification activities across education, land, and income groups (table 3.5). Furthermore, we roughly assess the returns to the respective activities

Table 3.4: Income shares of from different activities, by income quintiles

	Share of income from					
	Non-farm		Remittances		Farm	
	1991	1998	1991	1998	1991	1998
Income Quintile						
1	17,9	26,4	8,4	11,7	73,7	61,9
2	35,7	38,8	5,5	7,5	58,8	53,6
3	44,3	48,2	3,6	5,2	52,1	46,6
4	44,3	48,0	3,2	4,6	52,5	47,4
5	48,0	41,9	2,0	3,3	50,0	54,8
Source: Own Calculations.						

by computing annual growth rates for income earned from different activities per migrant or per household member engaged in the non-farm sector, respectively (table 3.6). The left column in table 3.6 shows the growth in total household income divided by the contributors, i.e. all household farm and non-farm workers plus migrants.

Table 3.5 shows that households significantly remove labour from the agricultural sector. The average number of migrants in a household doubles to 1.6 while the number of non-farm workers increases only slightly.

Highly-educated farm households have both more migrants and slightly more non-farm workers and these differences become more pronounced in 1998 for migration. Note that we have observed above that the share of highly educated households with migrants and non-farm workers even falls between 1991 and 1998. Furthermore, the income share from agriculture and remittances rises considerably for this group, whereas the non-farm income share declines. Possibly, the intensity of diversification[7] can be taken as a proxy for specialization and the results may

[7] The intensity of diversification is measured by the number of household members engaged in the particular strategy.

Table 3.5: Average number of household members engaged in diversification, 1991 and 1998.

Average number of household members working in						
	Non-farm		Migration		Farm	
	1991	1998	1991	1998	1991	1998
All	0,7	0,8	0,8	1,6	2,6	1,9
Highest level of education completed of hh head						
none	0,6	0,7	0,8	1,5	2,6	2,0
primary	0,7	0,8	0,9	1,6	2,4	1,9
secondary	0,8	1,0	0,9	1,8	2,4	1,9
higher	1,4	1,6	1,1	2,1	2,5	1,8
Land size (acres)						
0 - 1	0,8	1,0	0,8	1,5	2,7	2,0
1 - 2	0,5	0,8	0,8	1,6	2,6	2,0
2 - 4	0,5	0,7	0,9	1,6	2,4	1,9
4 -	0,4	0,6	1,0	1,9	2,1	1,6
Income Quintile						
1	0,2	0,4	0,7	1,3	3,1	2,0
2	0,6	0,7	0,8	1,3	3,0	2,1
3	0,8	0,9	0,8	1,7	2,7	1,9
4	0,8	1,1	0,9	1,7	2,4	1,9
5	0,8	1,0	0,9	2,0	1,8	1,7
Source: Own Calculations.						

Table 3.6: Growth of income per worker from different activities

	Growth of income per worker/migrant			
	All income 1991-1998	Non-farm income 1991-1998	Remittances 1991-1998	Farm income 1991-1998
All	1,0	-0,5	-0,2	4,7
Highest level of education completed of hh head				
none	-0,4	-2,3	-2,0	4,3
primary	1,9	-0,2	1,5	6,7
secondary	1,3	0,1	4,0	3,8
higher	5,7	3,4	29,8	15,8
Land size (acres)				
0 - 1	0,5	-0,4	-5,1	4,6
1 - 2	-0,3	-2,1	1,7	4,1
2 - 4	0,7	-0,3	4,4	2,4
4 -	2,1	0,3	11,8	4,3
Income Quintile				
1	-1,3	-0,9	-4,0	-1,6
2	0,8	0,1	-0,6	2,8
3	0,9	0,7	-2,1	1,9
4	0,6	-0,4	1,3	2,9
5	1,5	-0,9	1,3	5,7
Source: Own Calculations.				

hence indicate that these households are better at using their comparative advantages in migration.

With regard to land size, it is not too surprising that the average number of non-farm workers is lower for households with larger land holding - in line with the earlier findings on participation. These households also have less household members working on the farm, most likely because of the use of hired labour. Over time, no particular patterns of change arise.

The pattern for different income groups however changes quite considerably. The intensity of involvement into local non-farm activities is higher for richer households in both years, but the increase is strongest for the poorest income quintile. The average number of migrants in a household is also higher in richer households, but these differences are minor in 1991 and become much more pronounced by 1998. In contrast, the number of farm workers decreases much more for poorer than for richer households, who in general have fewer household members working on the farm. The average number of farm workers in a household in the lowest (highest) quintile declines from 3.1 (1.8) in 1991 to 2.0 (1.7) in 1998.

Even more dramatic changes can be observed for returns to different activities[8]. These results have to be interpreted cautiously, however, because income data is measured with error in household surveys. The re-

---

[8] The comparison of agricultural income growth rates between groups may be more reliable than the comparison of growth rates between different sources. It should be noted that the fairly high growth rates for agricultural income are somewhat at odds with previous findings on the performance of Ghanaian agriculture (e.g. McKay and Aryeetey, 2007). Furthermore, we would expect households to equate returns to different activities in their income portfolio, which again would not fit with some of the findings presented in the following.

sults can therefore at best show a tendency, and should not be interpreted as showing the exact size of returns. Overall, the returns per migrant or per local non-farm worker decrease, yet, with important differences between socio-economic groups. With regard to educational groups, very interesting patterns emerge. Overall, annual per worker (plus migrant) income growth is even negative for the non-educated - driven by high negative growth rates of returns to both diversification strategies and despite considerable growth of farm income per worker. Workers in households whose head has primary or secondary education fare better in particular regarding migration, but growth rates of income from local non-farm activities are close to zero. As for the non-educated, the reduction in the average number of household members working in the farm sector is accompanied by an increase in returns. The increase in returns from diversification is highest for those with higher than secondary education, whose returns rise by very high rates.

For different land size groups, similar patterns can be observed. Land-rich (with more than 4 acres) households' per worker income grows by the highest rate with remittances being the income component that grows most strongly. This group is also the only one with a slightly positive growth rate of returns from the non-farm sector. Particularly noteworthy is the strong correlation between land size and growth rate of remittances per migrant. Farm income per worker increases for all land-size groups alike.

These relationships between household assets and income growth are reflected in growth rates by income per capita quintiles. This implies that only for remittances per migrant a very clear pattern of growth rates can be detected. Remittances per migrant seem to decrease sharply for the lowest income per capita quintile. For higher income groups this growth rate is positive. Maybe somewhat unexpectedly, the picture is mixed for local non-farm activities. Only the third quintile experiences significant positive growth. For both the poorest and richest quintile income per worker from this source declines. Yet, the high income group has by far the highest annual growth rate of farm income per worker, leading to the highest overall growth rate of all income groups. In contrast, households in the lowest quintile are the only group that sees a decline in its farm income.

In sum, the descriptive statistics illustrate fairly large shifts in activity and income portfolios of rural households. Almost universally, rural households retreat from agricultural activities in the 1990s to engage more in local non-farm activities and/or to send migrants. These portfolio shifts seem to be driven by both motives for diversification - distress and opportunities. Asset-poor households, in terms of educational and/or land endowments, increasingly engage in the local non-farm sector and migration despite stagnating or, in some cases, dramatically falling returns from those activities. These households' diversification into activities with low or no entry barriers is hence very likely to be driven by desperation. In Table 3.1 we saw that the number of households with some assets, in particular in terms of formal (primary and secondary) education, increases significantly, as do their efforts to diversify. Although not as dramatic as for example for the non-educated, returns to diversification either stagnate or increase very modestly for this group. In contrast, asset-rich households seem to be able to diversify (or specialize) according to their comparative advantages. For example, some highly educated households even choose to engage in agriculture only. Returns from agriculture, however, measured as income per household member working on the farm, do not grow more slowly for asset-poor households.

The results provide some evidence that the non-agricultural labour market is indeed segmented. Furthermore, the fact that the number of households with primary and secondary education and their efforts to diversify rises, combined with negligible returns, especially in the non-farm sector, indicates the existence of vicious circles.

Taken together, diversification by poorer households and therefore diversification of the Ghanaian economy as a whole may indeed be driven by desperation rather than growing opportunities outside agriculture.

3.5 Assessing Change in a Multivariate Framework

The above descriptive analysis hints at the dichotomy of the observed diversifying behaviour. This section aims at identifying these different motivations in a multivariate framework. It aims also at identifying possible structural breaks regarding the determinants of diversification behaviour.

The decisions of the household to participate in either or both of the described diversification strategies cannot be analyzed separately. Diversification decisions are influenced by similar internal and external conditions a household faces and are certainly interdependent. Internal conditions include the composition of the household and its educational and asset endowment, in particular land. Important external conditions comprise access to infrastructure and markets. We estimate a seemingly unrelated probit model that accounts for the interdependence of decisions by allowing the disturbance terms to be correlated across equations (migration and non-farm participation). It is therefore superior to a separate probit estimation. We run the multivariate probit on the pooled cross-sections, including in a first stage time interactions for all explanatory variables. We then exclude time interactions that this regression renders insignificant and perform a Chow-Test on joint significance of these excluded variables. The results of this specification are reported in Table 3.7.

The seemingly bivariate probit model can be defined as follows:

$$y_1 = \alpha_1 + \beta_1 \mathbf{X}_1 + u_1 \tag{3.1}$$

$$y_2 = \alpha_2 + \beta_2 \mathbf{X}_2 + u_2 \tag{3.2}$$

$$E(u_1|X_1, X_2) = E(u_2|X_1, X_2) = 0 \tag{3.3}$$

$$E(var_1|X_1, X_2) = E(var_2|X_1, X_2) = \sigma \tag{3.4}$$

$$cov(u_1, u_2|X_1, X_2) = \rho \tag{3.5}$$

The dependent variables are observed as 1 if the household is participating in migration (y_1) or household members are working in the non-farm sectior (y_2).

Table 3.7: Pooled Seemingly Unrelated Bivariate Probit

	Migration	Non-farm
Log farm wealth	0.004 (0.004)	0.007* (0.004)
Prime-age adults	0.207*** (0.030)	0.007 (0.027)
Log farm land	0.151 (0.102)	0.367*** (0.102)
Log land per equivalent adult	-0.161 (0.102)	-0.465*** (0.100)
Age of head	0.004** (0.002)	-0.005** (0.002)
Head completed primary education	0.090 (0.078)	0.072 (0.069)
Head completed higher education	0.056 (0.049)	0.302*** (0.050)
Children 0-4	-0.119*** (0.025)	0.019 (0.027)
Children 5-14	-0.070*** (0.023)	-0.012 (0.021)
Adults 60 plus	0.069 (0.050)	-0.095* (0.052)
Perc. of female prime-age ad.	0.123 (0.075)	0.191*** (0.070)
Road Dummy	-0.168* (0.093)	0.109 (0.080)
Kilometres to next post off./telephone	-0.001 (0.001)	-0.009*** (0.003)
Perc. of hh with migrants per district	1.021*** (0.129)	-0.456** (0.183)
Population density	0.308* (0.170)	0.391 (0.294)
Dummy forest region	0.045 (0.064)	-0.136 (0.109)
Dummy savannah region	-0.199** (0.084)	-0.119 (0.146)
Dummy 1998 (d98)	-0.135 (0.111)	-0.275 (0.185)
Road * d98	0.232* (0.125)	
Kilometres to next post off./tel. *d98		0.008** (0.003)
Perc. of hh with migrants/district*d98		1.012*** (0.322)
Dummy forest region*d98		-0.262* (0.157)
Dummy savannah region*d98		-0.347* (0.209)
Constant	-1.062*** (0.146)	-0.184 (0.177)
Number of observations	4973	4973
Wald test of rho=0	chi2(1) = 0.105785, Prob > chi2 = 0.7450	

Source: Own Calculations.
Notes: The table reports marginal effects (in case of dummy variables from 0 to 1) and the corresponding standard errors. *0.1, **0.05, ***0.01 Significance level. Different specification with the eclusion of the variable "log land" because of a close correlation to "Log land per equivalent adult" were tested and showed no difference in the significance of the results for the other variables. Furthemore, when excluding one of the variables "Children 0-4, Children 5-14, Adults 60 plus, Prime-age adults" results do not change significantly as well.

Our regression results confirm some of the standard results from the literature on the determinants of diversification. Migrant networks are the most important determinant of migration. The supply of labour in the household is also an important explanatory variable: Engagement in migration is likelier the higher the number of ex-ante household members (migrants and household members).[9] Furthermore, population pressure is a significant determinant of migration. The higher population density the more household members seem to be pushed into migration. In the non-farm economy, involvement decreases with age of the household head and the household members as a whole. In addition, the more females of working age live on the farm, the more likely is participation in non-agricultural activities. Females often engage in petty trade, one of the most frequent forms of non-farm self-employment. Farm wealth is positively related to non-farm diversification. To a certain extent, farm wealth is of course endogenous to diversification, especially in the non-farm sector, as cash revenues can be used for agricultural investment. However, it is also possible that a higher farm wealth characterizes households with better access to the non-farm sector and migration through reduced entry barriers. Furthermore the rural savannah[10] and forest dummies are only significant for 1998 concerning non-farm diversification. This might reflect the effect a drought in these regions in 1998 causing less participation in the non-farm sector. Non-farm activities in economically underdeveloped regions are most likely closely linked to the

[9] The number of prime-age adults measures the number of ex-ante household members, i.e. before migration.

[10] The rural savannah region sends significantly fewer migrants. This might be due to the fact that important trade centers for the neighboring countries are present in these regions.

farm.

While most of the above results have been found in other studies as well, some findings merit particular consideration. In contrast to standard specifications, the choice model includes total land and land per adult equivalent separately. Total farm land may be an important asset that allows the household to overcome entry barriers, for example by providing collateral. Farm land per equivalent adult instead measures whether the household is able to supply household members adequately with food and land. In fact we find that the likelihood of diversifying in the non-farm sector increases (concave) with total land farmed.[11] In contrast, the less land is available per adult equivalent the more the family is pushed into non-farm diversification.[12]

As commonly found, completed vocational and tertiary education seems to be a valuable asset for entering the non-farm economy. In contrast, migration is not a strategy of households whose head has higher education.

Considering infrastructure we find two distinct effects. We find a negative relationship between migration and existence of a road. A good infrastructure implies that agricultural produce can be easily carried to markets. Furthermore, demand is higher than in remote regions making migration less necessary. Related to this, infrastructure might be an indicator for better opportunities in non-farm sector participation. The amount of kilometres to next public telephone and post office, that is the

11 This variable however would be clearly endogenous to migration if we included the number of equivalent adults after migration. We therefore again calculate the number of ex-ante adult equivalents by including migrants.

12 The total effect of land farmed has to be calculated as follows: $\beta_3 + \beta_4 * 1/adultequivalents = 0.25$

remoteness of the place of living, is related negatively to the likelihood of participation in the non-farm economy. The time dummy interaction shows that remoteness has a positive effect on non-farm diversification in 1998. Several possible theories might explain this relation. One explanation is that remote households are pushed into desperation-led diversification in 1998. Another possibility is that increasing competition in the non-farm sector leads to this positive correlation.[13] The growth of the non-farm sector combined with the growth of labour supply through migration and therefore growth in competition lead to a spread in non-farm activities to more remote areas. These considerations are backed by the finding that road availability decreases the probability of migration, but in 1998 the inverse effect is found. This underlines the hypothesis that infrastructure is a proxy for opportunities, but also competition in the local farm and non-farm sector.

An equally interesting change in the effect between the years is found when considering migration networks.[14] Migrant networks on average decrease the probability of non-farm diversification. Most likely this captures the effect of missing labour. In 1998, however, migrant networks foster participation in non-farm activities. This might be explained by a significant increase in remittances sent home between 1991 and 1998 or by returning migrants that invest their savings by founding micro-enterprises.

[13] A significant improvement in infrastructure did not happen since the mean kilometres to next post office or telephone increased between 1991 and 1998.

[14] The more common migration is in the district the more likely the household is to send away migrants. Migration networks significantly reduce entry barriers to migration as migration becomes less costly and the probability of success of the migrant might increase.

As the relationship between diversification outcomes and explanatory variables appears to remain fairly stable, a look at changes in diversification determinants in the in the course of the 1990s may be informative. Table C.1 in appendix C provides descriptive statistics for the right-hand side variables of the above regression. To quantify the impact of those changes on diversification behaviour, we "endow" the average 1991 farmer with specific characteristics of the average 1998 farmer and calculate counterfactual probabilities. Table 3.8 hence shows the effects of selected important explanatory variables on participation in different diversification strategies.

Table 3.8: Illustrative simulations of contributions of different determinants to changes in diversification outcomes, 1991 to 1998

	Probability of diversifying into	
	Non-farm	Migration
Average 1991 farmer	54,7	55,9
Average 1998 farmer	61,8	67,8
Percentage point change in probability (compared to average 1991 farmer)		
with 1998 land endowments	1,8	0,7
with 1998 demographic characteristics	-0,3	5,3
with 1998 migrant network	17,9	1,9
with 1998 infrastructure	0,0	8,9
Source: Own Calculations.		

The descriptive statistics in Table C.1 in appendix C illustrate the significant demographic change between 1991 and 1998. The number of prime age adults increases significantly. In Table 8 we can also see the results of the acreage expansion that resulted in more farm land in 1998. However, the increase was rather small in mean. Some of the progenies of the FCUBE initiative are reflected in increased primary school completion rates. As mentioned above the infrastructural investment programs were modestly successful, but road density increased slightly.

Allocating the mean farm household of 1991 the average migrant networks of 1998 has the most sizeable effect on participation. Participation rates in non-farm diversification and involvement in migration significantly increase. When we look at the combined effect of household demographic composition on changes in participation we find a smaller but also sizable effect on migration. The likelihood of participating in migration strategies rises as the number of prime-age adults rises. Allocating to the average farmer of 1991 the infrastructure of 1998 significantly increases the probability of participation in migration.

The results confirm that governmental reforms had only minor effects on household behaviour, whereas the demographic transition and former migration decisions and therefore also preferences of households had the most pronounced impact.

The analysis suggests that the influence of most of the drivers of diversification behaviour do not change dramatically. In other words, a household whose head has completed secondary education is equally likely to diversify in 1991 and 1998. Yet, there are many more of such households in 1998. We find two notable structural breaks regarding the determinants of diversification decisions. The effect of migration networks and infrastructure appears to change between 1991 and 1998. The impact of migrant networks points to complementarities between migration and non-farm sector participation.

In sum, the regression results hint towards the existence of dichotomous diversification strategies. These differences imply the existence of segmented local non-farm markets.

Concerning migration we find that remoteness and population pressure act as a push-factor. This is a sign for desperation-led diversification. We find no evidence that higher education fosters migration. The only hint at opportunity-led migration is the economic significance of migrant networks as explanatory variable.

In the non-farm sector the dichotomy becomes perhaps much clearer. The positive influence of higher education and the distinct positive effect of migrant networks in 1998 on non-farm participation are in line with opportunity-led diversification. The negative influence of land per adult equivalent instead shows that desperation-led motivations also play a role.

3.6 Distributional and Poverty Implications

In this section we investigate the poverty and inequality implications of the above described change in income-portfolios. In 1991, about 65 percent of rural households in Ghana were poor using a 900,000 Cedis poverty line (table 3.9).[15] Poverty dropped by 16 percentage points to 49 percent in 1998. However, this sharp decline in poverty was accompanied by an increase, albeit small, in the Gini index from 0.329 to 0.334.

[15] Headcount and Gini indices are computed from expenditure per capita percentiles, which of course may lead to inaccuracies when compared to figures based on primary data. See also the notes on Table 10.

Table 3.9: Poverty and distributional implications of income growth by source, illustrative simulations

	Gini	Headcount
Initial levels	32,9	65,0
Percentage point changes		
overall 1991-98	0,5	-16,0
only non-farm growth	-2,4	-6,0
only remittances growth	0,4	-2,0
only farm growth	3,5	-9,0
Source: Own Calculations.		

For the experiment we successively substitute non-farm income, remittance income, and farm income of 1991 with the 1998 values.[16] Non-farm income growth has a significant reducing effect on inequality (2.4 percentage points) and more pronounced on poverty (6 percentage points). Allocating the mean farmer of 1991 remittances of 1998 has no effect on inequality, while poverty declines by 2 percentage points. The growth of farm income alone is associated with a substantial reduction in poverty (9 percentage points) and a considerable increase in inequality (3.5 percentage points). Growth incidence curves (Figure 1[17]) give a more detailed picture of whether the poor benefited overall from economic development in the three sectors. Broadly, expenditure growth has been fairly equally distributed. Yet, the growth incidence curve for farm income growth illustrates that agricultural income growth is around nil or even negative in the lowest expenditure quintile while it reaches around 5 percent for the richest rural households. Poorer households compensate for the lack of

[16] This is done by calculating expenditure and income data by vintile and then merging the 1991 and 1998 data sets.

[17] Source: Authors' calculations. Note: The graphs plot per adult equivalent income growth by source. Income sources are calculated as in table 3.9. The graphs are based on smoothed curves on vintile averages. More details are available from the authors.

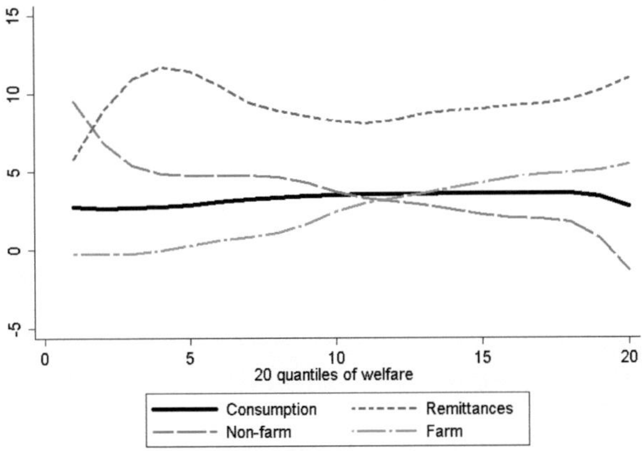

Figure 3.1: Growth rates of adult equivalent income by source (annual growth rates).

agricultural income growth by venturing into both non-farm employment and migration. Non-farm income grows by almost 10 percent annually for the poorest. Remittance income increases very strongly for all income groups with a peak in the growth rate around the 20th percentile of the distribution. Non-farm employment hence appears to be more accessible to the poorest of the poor than migration.

The above counterfactual experiments illustrate the sizeable shifts in rural income composition across the income distribution. As non-farm income growth apparently benefits the poor more than the rich, one might now be inclined to claim that non-farm income growth is pro-poor: If it had not been for non-farm growth, the poor might not have seen the recorded welfare improvements. This can also be said of remittances income although its overall contribution to rural households' income is still relatively low.

3.7 Conclusion

We find that rural households increasingly diversify their livelihoods by both increased migration and more local non-farm employment. Our key finding is that households with a low non-labour asset-base are increasingly diversified and poor. Asset-poor households, which account for an important share of the rural population, are hence likely to be "pushed" into activities off the farm to meet subsistence needs. While the returns to diversification activities for these households appear to become under pressure, those earned by asset-rich, in particular highly-educated, households increase, often quite substantially. These households are hence the only group that successfully diversifies or specialises by picking those activities the household is relatively good at.

These developments are reflected in our incidence analysis of income growth by source. The falling returns to diversification activities are more than compensated for through higher participation by poor households. Hence, the share of income from non-agricultural sources increases considerably and, in fact, drives income growth of the poorest, whose income from agriculture stagnates. In particular, local non-farm income growth has mainly benefited poorer households. While this may be true from a static perspective, our analysis may also give reasons to be concerned, as high non-farm growth rates are achieved through allocating more labour to the local non-farm sector as well as migration and not by improved "diversification productivity". In contrast, farm growth has been the most important source of income growth for richer income groups, thereby increasing inequality. Yet, because of its importance for all rural households it still has a considerable impact on poverty reduction.

In sum, rural structural change that eventually results from household diversification decisions seems to be driven to a large extent by desperation rather than new opportunities that only the richest households seem to be able to grasp. Our analysis shows that Ghana's rural areas, contrary to common beliefs, have seen major economic transformation that may not be evident from national accounts statistics or from averages based on household survey data. This transformation apparently has very different welfare implications across socio-economic groups and tends to biased in favour of richer income groups.

This probably does not imply that diversification cannot provide a pathway out of poverty. There still is a positive correlation between income per capita and diversification, but it appears to become weaker. The paper also sheds some light on why this is happening, i.e. the drivers of the changes in diversification behaviour. The regression analysis suggests that changes have a lot to do with changes in households' endowments and less with structural breaks in the participation decision. In particular, the expansion of education has certainly enabled or motivated more individuals to engage in local non-farm activities. This may also explain why the phenomenon of stagnating returns to activities out of agriculture is not confined to the asset-poor, it also holds - although to a lesser extent - for the increasing number of better educated households.

Access to roads and markets plays a key role in changing diversification patterns and apparently the migrant networks increasingly foster local non-farm sector growth in migrants' areas of origin. Experiences from emerging market economies showed the importance of investing in infrastructure and the investment climate although possibilities to intervene in remote rural are constrained (World Bank, 2007). Migrant networks therefore pose the chance to fill some of the gap. Interestingly the paper showed that only the highest income groups were able to profit from agricultural growth. It would therefore be important to analyse why this happened and how the poor can be enabled to participate in agricultural growth.

The results presented here call for a detailed analysis of the rural labour market in Ghana and Sub-Saharan Africa in general. Unfortunately data constraints made it impossible to analyse the segmentation of and structural change on the labour market in detail. It would be more favourable to know in which segments of the rural non-farm economy the poor are concentrated and which segments experience more turn-over. This would be indispensable for identifying policy implications. Such an analysis should also contribute to a better understanding of the transformation processes triggered by structural adjustment in largely rural and hence agricultural African economies.

Chapter 4

Conclusion and Future Research

This study analyses three particular topics of migration. The second chapter considers effects of migration on the recipient country. This chapter investigates the growth impact of past immigration or settlement and its interaction with ethnic diversity. The results highlight that the effects of ethnic diversity are complex and that there seems to exist an "Acemoglu"-type advantageous impact of ethnic diversity in countries created partially through settlement in the past.

Furthermore, in a world where migrant flows are severely restricted massive inmigration that changes ethnic diversity significantly seems unlikely to exist in many countries. It is therefore important to highlight the positive growth enhancing effects found in industrialized countries generated by a small community of migrants.

The following two chapters analyse the effects and the role of migration in the sending country. The third chapter highlights that adverse behavioral effects on effort exist at the micro-level which at least to some extent crowd out potential poverty reducing effects of remittances. It delivers also an explanation why other studies found that a potential Dutch Disease effect of remittances at the macro-level might be minor. Nevertheless evidence on the welfare-enhancing effects of remittances is found as remittances tend to insure the household at least partially against shocks.

The fourth chapter stresses the importance of migration as diversification strategy of the household in the process of structural change. Furthermore, it is shown that the asset-poor are likely to diversify out of agriculture for the reason of desperation. Only the asset-rich are able to reap the benefits of migration and non-farm sector participation.

In sum, it can be concluded that migration is an important instrument for households to adjust in the process of development. For the household this strategy is necessary and optimal. From a policy perspective, however, the detrimental effects of migration in the sending country have to be taken into account. This does not mean that migration should be restricted, but that governments have to take measures that reduce the need for migration. Remittances are often presented as being a substitute for aid. The disincenitves created by remittances due to informational assymetries, however, narrow the potential poverty reducing effect.

Massive out-migration - internal or international - indicates the existence of obstacles to development in sending regions and countries. In order to ensure an advantageous effect of remittances governments should invest in infrastructure that gives rise to local opportunities of diversification and growth. Furthermore, this ensures that migrants regain confidence in their home country or government and return eventually.

The above research brings up several potential future research questions. Most of them can only be analysed if better data become available. As has been stated by many researchers, the data on migration is far from being ideal for analysing migration on the micro-economic level in the sending country. Most surveys provide too few information on the situation of migrants in their former as well as new place of residence. Specifically, it would be interesting to have more detailed data on the labour market migrants work in and have been working in, in order to assess the success of migrants. A detailed labour market analyses allows to assess the extent of structural change and investigate the characteristics of this turnround more deeply.

Furthermore, surveys provide far from complete data on transfers in cash or in kind a household receives. For the purpose of this study it would also have been important, to have more detailed information on other informal insurance schemes a household is possibly engaged in. It would be interesting to be able to judge the importance of remittances compared to other insurance options of the household.

Chapter 3 shows that migrants are not only potential insurers of the household, but are also petitioners. It would be important to investigate more deeply in which case the migrant is more likely to be a petitioner, that is, in which case migration is no effective diversification strategy of the household.

There is a lack of panel data in order to assess the behavioral and welfare effects of remittances in a wider country setting. On the welfare side, interesting future research would analyse time use in the recipient family. If less time is spent working, more time is spend inside the household, for example, on child care. Even more important would be to determine whether remittances allow the household to overcome entry barriers into the non-farm sector. This requires data on the date of entry in the non-farm sector and also possible exit. Furthermore meso-level characteristics of the region or village where the recipient is living have to be taken into account. These variables should measure potential opportunities to invest a recipient faces.

As McKenzie and Sasin (2007) have highlighted, a further interesting field of future research could be a comparative analysis of migration policies of sending countries. An analysis would comprise the effectiveness of policies, as well as the welfare costs and benefits of these policies. Concerning remittances, policy implications for sending countries have to be formulated with caution, as remittances are private money.

Appendix A

Table A.1: Variable Definitions - Chapter 2

Growth: Growth rate of real per capita GDP, World Bank
Initial Income: Log of real GDP per capita measured at
the beginning of each decade (1960, 1970, 1980, 1990), Penn World Tables
Schooling: Log of 1 + average years of school attainment
measured at the beginning f each decade, updated Barro and Lee (1993)
Assassinations: Number of assassinations per thousand
populations, decade average, updated Banks (1994)
Financial Depth: Ratio of liquid liabilities of the financial
system to GDP, decade average, updated King and Levine (1993b)
Black Market Premium: Log of 1 + black market premium,
decade average, updated World Bank (1991) and Pick's Currency yearbook (various years)
Fiscal Surplus/GDP: Central government surplus as percentage
of GDP, local currency and current prices, decade average, International Financial and Government Finance Statistics (IMF)
Telephones per people: Log of telephones per thousand people,
World Development Indicators,World Bank (various years)
Ethnic: Index of ethnolinguistic fractionalisation, Encyclopedia
Britannica (2001), CIA World Factbook (2000), Levinson (1998), Minority Rights Group International (1997)
Initial Investment/GDP: Investment Share of Real GDP per
capita (Laspeyres) (constant price entries) Penn World Tables, measured at the beginning of each decade
Investment/GDP: Investment Share of Real GDP per capita
(Laspeyres) (constant price entries) Penn World Tables, decade average
Kaufmann, Kraay and Zoido-Lobaton-Index: Aggregate Index
measuring goverance in various dimensions of voice and accountability, Kaufmann, Kraay and Zoido-Lobaton (1999)
Immigration Dummy: Dummy variable: 1 if several different
ethnic groups (descendants of migrants from non-neighbouring countries) make up more than 5 percent the population

Table A.2: Countries Included

Countries Included	
AFGHANISTAN	CAMBODIA
ANGOLA	KIRIBATI
ALBANIA	ST. KITTS AND NEVIS
ARGENTINA	KOREA, REPUBLIC OF
ANTIGUA AND BARBUDA	LAO PEOPLE'S DEMOCRATIC REPUBLIC
AUSTRALIA	LEBANON
AUSTRIA	LIBERIA
BURUNDI	LIBYA
BELGIUM	SRI LANKA
BENIN	LESOTHO
BANGLADESH	LUXEMBOURG
BULGARIA	MOROCCO
BAHAMAS, THE	MADAGASCAR
BELIZE	MEXICO
BOLIVIA	MALI
BRAZIL	MALTA
BARBADOS	MONGOLIA
BRUNEI	MOZAMBIQUE
BHUTAN	MAURITANIA
MYANMAR	MAURITIUS
BOTSWANA	MALAWI
CENTRAL AFRICAN REPUBLIC	MALAYSIA
CANADA	NAMIBIA
SWITZERLAND	NIGER
CHILE	NIGERIA
CHINA	NICARAGUA
COTE D'IVOIRE	NETHERLANDS
CAMEROON	NORWAY
CONGO	NEPAL
COLOMBIA	NEW ZEALAND
CAPE VERDE	PAKISTAN
COSTA RICA	PANAMA
CYPRUS	PERU
DJIBOUTI	PHILIPPINES
DOMINICA	PAPUA NEW GUINEA
DENMARK	POLAND
DOMINICAN REPUBLIC	PORTUGAL
ALGERIA	PARAGUAY
ECUADOR	ROMANIA
EGYPT	RWANDA
SPAIN	SUDAN
ETHIOPIA	SENEGAL

FINLAND	SINGAPORE
FIJI	SOLOMON ISLANDS
FRANCE	SIERRA LEONE
GABON	SWEDEN
UNITED KINGDOM	SWAZILAND
GHANA	SEYCHELLES
GUINEA	EL SALVADOR
GAMBIA, THE	SOMALIA
GUINEA-BISSAU	SURINAME
EQUATORIAL GUINEA	SYRIAN ARAB REPUBLIC
GREECE	CHAD
GRENADA	TOGO
GUATEMALA	THAILAND
GUYANA	TONGA
HONG KONG	TRINIDAD AND TOBAGO
HONDURAS	TUNISIA
HAITI	TURKEY
HUNGARY	TANZANIA
BURKINA FASO	UGANDA
INDONESIA	URUGUAY
INDIA	UNITED STATES
IRELAND	VENEZUELA
ICELAND	VANUATU
ISRAEL	VIETNAM
ITALY	WESTERN SAMOAY
JAMAICA	UGOSLAVIA, FEDERAL REPUBLIC
JORDAN	SOUTH AFRICA
JAPAN	ZAIRE
KENYA	ZAMBIA
	ZIMBABWE

Table A.3: Sub-Saharan African Countries Included

Country-Year Combinations				
Country	1960	1970	1980	1990
ANGOLA	x	x	x	x
BURUNDI	x	x	x	x
BENIN	x	x	x	x
BOTSWANA	x	x	x	x
CENTRAL AFRICAN REPUBLIC	x	x	x	x
COTE D'IVOIRE	x	x	x	x
CAMEROON	x	x	x	x
CONGO	x	x	x	x
CAPE VERDE				x
DJIBOUTI				x
ETHIOPIA	x	x	x	x
GABON	x	x	x	x
GHANA	x	x	x	x
GUINEA				x
GAMBIA, THE	x	x	x	x
GUINEA-BISSAU		x	x	x
EQUATORIAL GUINEA				x
BURKINA FASO	x	x	x	x
KENYA	x	x	x	x
LIBERIA	x	x	x	x
LESOTHO	x	x	x	x
MADAGASCAR	x	x	x	x
MALI	x	x	x	x
MOZAMBIQUE			x	x
MAURITANIA	x	x	x	x
MAURITIUS	x	x	x	x
MALAWI	x	x	x	x
NAMIBIA				x
NIGER	x	x	x	x
NIGERIA	x	x	x	x
RWANDA	x	x	x	x
SUDAN	x	x	x	x
SENEGAL	x	x	x	x
SIERRA LEONE	x	x	x	x
SOMALIA	x	x	x	x
SWAZILAND	x	x	x	x
SEYCHELLES				x
CHAD	x	x	x	x
TOGO	x	x	x	x
TANZANIA	x	x	x	x

UGANDA	x	x	x	x
SOUTH AFRICA	x	x	x	x
ZAIRE	x	x	x	x
ZAMBIA	x	x	x	x
ZIMBABWE	x	x	x	x

Table A.4: Latin-American Countries Included

Country-Year Combinations				
Country	1960	1970	1980	1990
ARGENTINA	x	x	x	x
ANTIGUA AND BARBUDA				x
BAHAMAS, THE				x
BELIZE				x
BOLIVIA	x	x	x	x
BRAZIL	x	x	x	x
BARBADOS	x	x	x	x
CHILE	x	x	x	x
COLOMBIA	x	x	x	x
COSTA RICA	x	x	x	x
DOMINICA	x	x	x	x
DOMINICAN REPUBLIC				x
ECUADOR	x	x	x	x
GRENADA				x
GUATEMALA	x	x	x	x
GUYANA		x	x	x
HONDURAS	x	x	x	x
HAITI	x	x	x	x
JAMAICA	x	x	x	x
ST. KITTS AND NEVIS				x
MEXICO	x	x	x	x
NICARAGUA	x	x	x	x
PANAMA	x	x	x	x
PERU	x	x	x	x
PARAGUAY	x	x	x	x
EL SALVADOR	x	x	x	x
SURINAME		x	x	x
TRINIDAD AND TOBAGO	x	x	x	x
URUGUAY	x	x	x	x
VENEZUELA	x	x	x	x

Table A.5: Countries Included - Rest of the World

Country-Year Combinations				
Country	1960	1970	1980	1990
ALBANIA	x	x	x	x
AUSTRALIA	x	x	x	x
AUSTRIA	x	x	x	x
BELGIUM	x	x	x	x
BANGLADESH	x	x	x	x
BULGARIA				x
BRUNEI				x
BHUTAN				x
MYANMAR	x	x	x	x
CANADA	x	x	x	x
SWITZERLAND	x	x	x	x
CHINA				x
CYPRUS	x	x	x	x
DENMARK	x	x	x	x
ALGERIA	x	x	x	x
EGYPT	x	x	x	x
SPAIN	x	x	x	x
FINLAND	x	x	x	x
FIJI	x	x	x	x
FRANCE	x	x	x	x
UNITED KINGDOM	x	x	x	x
GREECE	x	x	x	x
HONG KONG	x	x	x	x
HUNGARY				x
INDONESIA	x	x	x	x
INDIA	x	x	x	x
IRELAND	x	x	x	x
ICELAND	x	x	x	x
ISRAEL	x	x	x	x
ITALY	x	x	x	x
JORDAN		x	x	x
JAPAN	x	x	x	x
CAMBODIA				x
KIRIBATI				x
KOREA, REPUBLIC OF	x	x	x	x
LAO PEOPLE'S DEMOCRATIC REPUBLIC				x
LEBANON				x
SRI LANKA	x	x	x	x
LUXEMBOURG	x	x	x	x
MOROCCO	x	x	x	x

MALTA	x	x	x	x
MONGOLIA				x
MALAYSIA	x	x	x	x
NETHERLANDS	x	x	x	x
NORWAY	x	x	x	x
NEPAL		x		x
NEW ZEALAND	x	x	x	x
PAKISTAN	x	x	x	x
PHILIPPINES	x	x	x	x
PAPUA NEW GUINEA	x	x	x	x
POLAND				x
PORTUGAL	x	x	x	x
ROMANIA				x
SINGAPORE	x	x	x	x
SOLOMON ISLANDS				x
SWEDEN	x	x	x	x
SYRIAN ARAB REPUBLIC	x	x	x	x
THAILAND	x	x	x	x
TONGA				x
TUNISIA	x	x	x	x
TURKEY	x	x	x	x
UNITED STATES	x	x	x	x
VIET NAM				x
VANUATU				x

Table A.6: Unrestricted SUR Model.

	Dependent Variable: Growth rate 1960-1999	
Variable	Coefficient	t-Statistic
Dummy for the 1960s	-0.267	-1.15
Dummy for the 1970s	-0.396**	-2.14**
Dummy for the 1980s	-0.167	-1.45
Dummy for the 1990s	0.103	-0.65
1960s		
Sub-Saharan Africa	-0.019**	-1.94**
Latin America & Caribbean	-0.024*	-3.68*
Log of initial income	0.091	1.54
Log of initial income squared	-0.007	-1.83
Log of schooling	0.013	1.50
Assassinations	46.595	0.94
Financial Depth	0.0001	0.01
Black Market Premium	-0.0187	-1.34
Fiscal surplus/GDP	0.084	0.78
Log of telephones per people	0.011	0.99
Ethnic	**0.000**	**0.05**

Adj R2	0.29	
Observations	38	
	1970s	
Sub-Saharan Africa	-0.005	-0.80
Latin America & Caribbean	-0.014**	-2.23**
Log of initial income	0.138*	2.92*
Log of initial income squared	-0.011*	-3.65*
Log of schooling	0.002	0.34
Assassinations	-22.564	-1.52
Financial Depth	0.009	0.92
Black Market Premium	-0.028*	-3.06*
Fiscal surplus/GDP	0.197*	3.19*
Log of telephones per people	0.038*	4.25*
Ethnic	**0.002**	**0.21**
Adj R2	0.51	
Observations	67	
	1980s	
Sub-Saharan Africa	-0.012**	-1.98**
Latin America & Caribbean	-0.019*	-3.76*
Log of initial income	0.061**	2.09**
Log of initial income squared	-0.005*	-2.75*
Log of schooling	0.004	0.61
Assassinations	-21.280**	-2.19**
Financial Depth	0.016**	2.02**
Black Market Premium	-0.009***	-1.82***
Fiscal surplus/GDP	0.121*	3.46*
Log of telephones per people	0.024*	2.63*
Ethnic	**-0.002**	**-0.22**
Adj R2	0.48	
Observations	74	
	1990s	
Sub-Saharan Africa	-0.01*	-2.63*
Latin America & Caribbean	-0.008	-1.34
Log of initial income	-0.005	-0.13
Log of initial income squared	-0.001	-0.42
Log of schooling	0.005	0.58
Assassinations	-72.156**	-1.99**
Financial Depth	0.008	0.94
Black Market Premium	-0.020**	-2.28**
Fiscal surplus/GDP	0.165*	2.58*
Log of telephones per people	0.015	1.25
Ethnic	**-0.018****	**-1.93****
Adj R2	0.24	
Observations	78	

Total Pool No. Obs.	257

Source: Own Calculations. *0.1, **0.05, ***0.01 Significance level

Table A.7: SUR Model including Kaufmann, Kraay and Zoido-Lobaton Index - Robustness.

Dependent Variable: Growth rate 1960-1989	
Variable	OLS
Sub-Saharan Africa	-0.013 (0.010)
Latin America & Caribbean	-0.008 (0.008)
Log of initial income	0.016 (0.047)
Log of initial income squared	-0.002 (0.003)
Log of schooling	0.012 (0.012)
Assassinations	-73.870 (43.195)*
Financial Depth	0.007 (0.010)
Black Market Premium	-0.026 (0.014)*
Fiscal surplus/GDP	0.139 (0.084)
Log of telephones per people	0.013 (0.015)
Ethnic	-0.023 (0.012)*
Constant	0.010 (0.197)
Observations	65
R-squared	0.39

Source: Own Calculations. Note: t-stats in parentheses *0.1, **0.05, ***0.01 Significance level.

Table A.8: Unrestricted SUR Model including Investment.

	Dependent Variable: Growth rate 1960-1999	
Variable	Coefficient	t-Statistic
Dummy for the 1960s	-0,092	-0,64
Dummy for the 1970s	-0,335*	-2,09
Dummy for the 1980s	-0,201**	-1,86
Dummy for the 1990s	0,017	0,11
1960s		
Africa	-0,021	-1,35
Latin America	-0,013***	-2,73
Log of initial income	0,037	0,97
Log of initial income squared	-0,003	-1,19
Log of schooling	0,013**	2,07
Investment as perc. of GDP	0,001**	2,15
Ethnic	-0,005	-0,55

Ethnic*SSA	0,017	0,71
Adj R2	0,19	
Observations	76	
	1970s	
Africa	0,050***	2,78
Latin America	-0,011**	-1,96
Log of initial income	0,099**	2,38
Log of initial income squared	-0,007***	-2,55
Log of schooling	0,005	0,74
Investment as perc. of GDP	0,001***	2,83
Ethnic	-0,006	-0,56
Ethnic*SSA	-0,096***	-3,60
Adj R2	0,32	
Observations	82	
	1980s	
Africa	0,001	0,05
Latin America	-0,021***	-4,34
Log of initial income	0,055**	2,02
Log of initial income squared	-0,004**	-2,30
Log of schooling	0,010*	1,82
Investment as perc. of GDP	0,002***	5,26
Ethnic	-0,010	-1,17
Ethnic*SSA	-0,009	-0,45
Adj R2	0,49	
Observations	88	
	1990s	
Africa	-0,001	-0,09
Latin America	-0,006	-1,20
Log of initial income	0,004	0,11
Log of initial income squared	-0,001	-0,33
Log of schooling	0,005	0,71
Investment as perc. of GDP	0,001***	2,69
Ethnic	-0,007	-0,72
Ethnic*SSA	-0,023	-0,94
Adj R2	0,19	
Observations	92	
No. Obs.	338	

Source: Own Calculations. *0.1, **0.05, ***0.01 Significance level

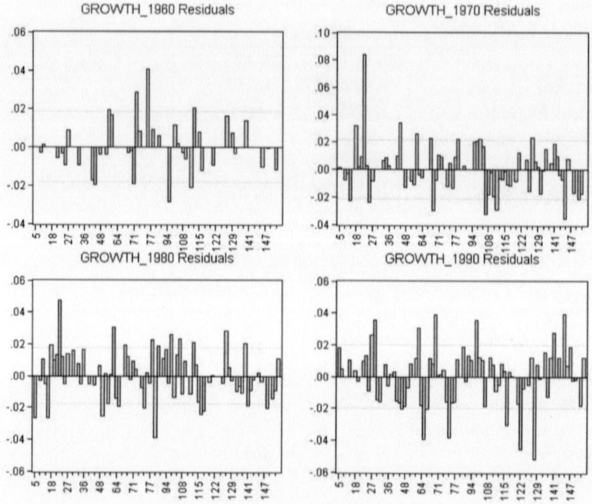

Figure A.1: Residual Plot: 1990s Effect

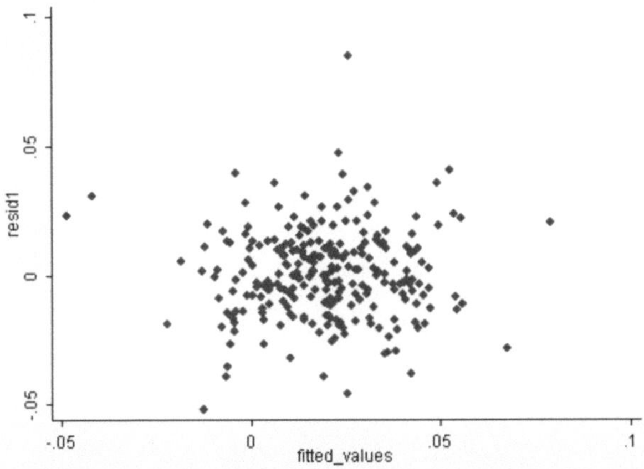

Figure A.2: Residual Plot 2: 1990s Effect

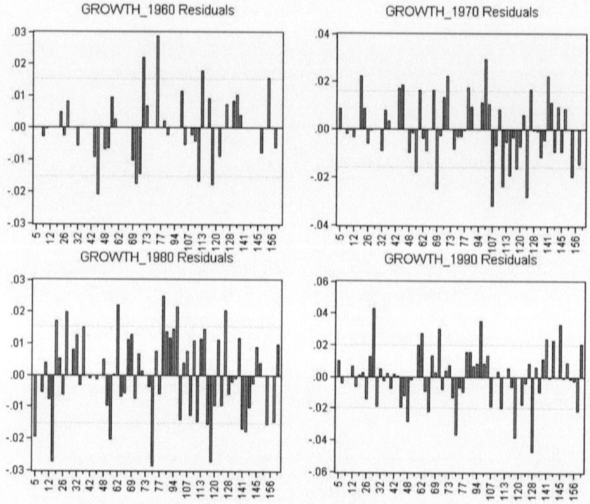

Figure A.3: Residual Plot: Unrestricted SUR Model including Kaufmann, Kraay and Zoido-Lobaton Index

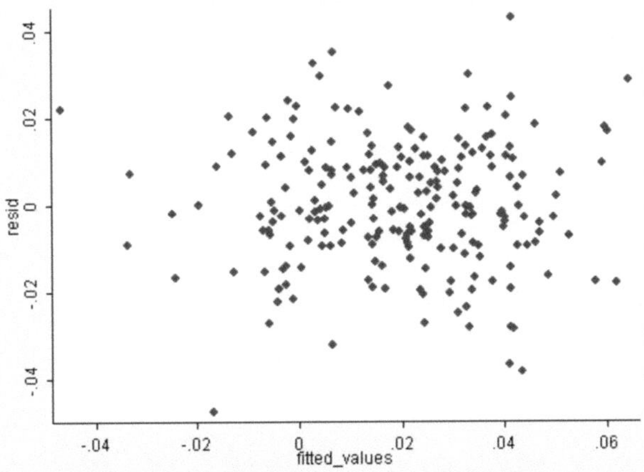

Figure A.4: Residual Plot 2: Unrestricted SUR Model including Kaufmann, Kraay and Zoido-Lobaton Index

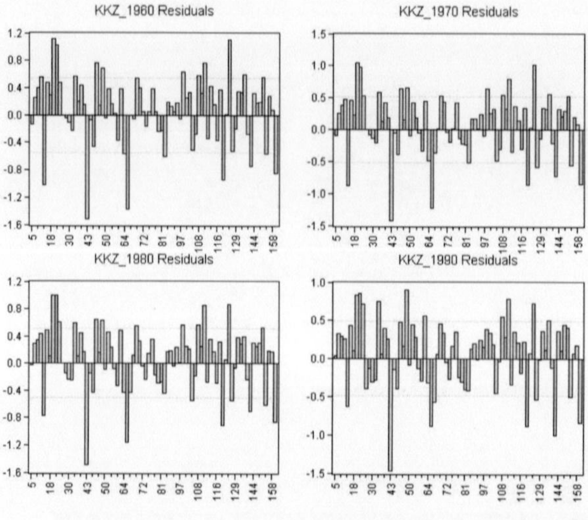

Figure A.5: Residual Plot: Indirect Effect of Fractionalisation on Good Governance

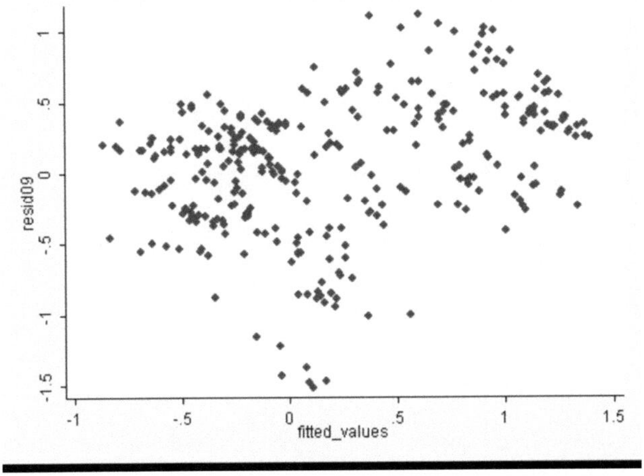

Figure A.6: Residual Plot 2: Indirect Effect of Fractionalisation on Good Governance

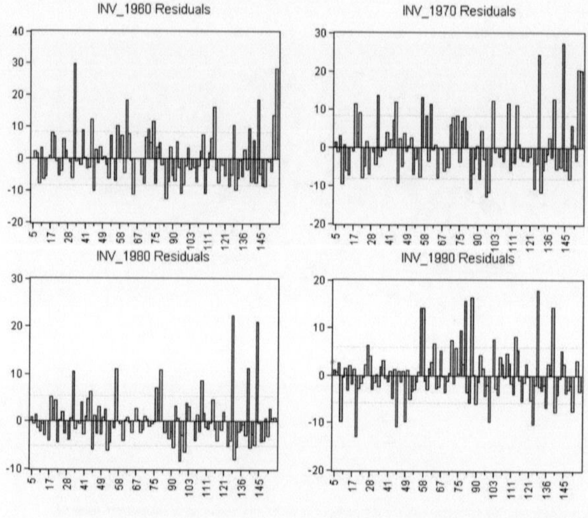

Figure A.7: Residual Plot: Indirect Effect of Fragmentation in SSA - Decade Specific

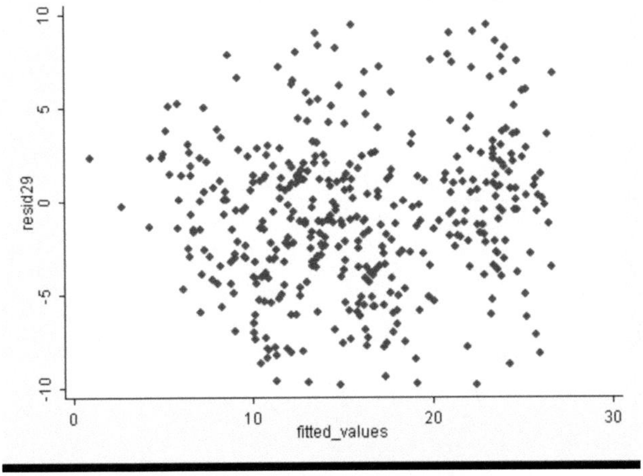

Figure A.8: Residual Plot 2: Indirect Effect of Fragmentation in SSA - Decade Specific

Table A.9: Immigration Country Definition

Countries Included
ARGENTINA
AUSTRALIA
BAHAMAS
BOLIVIA
BRAZIL
BARBADOS
BRUNEI
CANADA
CHILE
COLOMBIA
COSTA RICA
DOMINICA
DOMINICAN REPUBLIC
ECUADOR
FIJI
GRENADA
GUATEMALA
GUYANA
HAITI
HONDURAS
ISRAEL
JAMAICA
MEXICO
MALAYSIA
NAMIBIA
NETHERLANDS
NEW ZEALAND
NICARAGUA
PANAMA
PERU
PUERTO RICO
PARAGUAY
SINGAPORE
EL SALVADOR
SAO TOME AND PRINCIPE
SURINAME
THAILAND
TRINIDAD AND TOBAGO
URUGUAY
UNITED STATES
UNITED KINGDOM
VENEZUELA
SOUTH AFRICA

Table A.10: Comparison Alesina et al. with our Results

Dependent Variable: Growth rate 1960-1989		
Variable	1	2
Dummy for the 1960s	-0.233***	-0.166*
	(-2.34)	(-1.73)
Dummy for the 1970s	-0.227***	-0.163*
	(-2.28)	(-1.70)
Dummy for the 1980s	-0.243***	-0.179*
	(-2.45)	(-1.88)
Dummy for Sub-Saharan Africa	-0.017***	-0.013***
	(-3.11)	(-2.75)
Dummy for Latin America & Caribbean	-0.015***	-0.017***
	(-4.14)	(-4.46)
Log of initial income	0.081***	0.067***
	(3.23)	(2.76)
Log of initial income squared	-0.007***	-0.006***
	(-3.98)	(-3.66)
Log of schooling	**0.009***	**0.005**
	(1.85)	**(0.96)**
Assassinations	-23.705***	-17.985*
	(-2.58)	(-1.95)
Financial Depth	0.013**	0.011**
	(2.12)	(1.99)
Black Market Premium	-0.018***	-0.015***
	(-4.10)	(-3.45)
Fiscal surplus/GDP	0.165***	0.11***
	(4.45)	(3.64)
Log of telephones per worker	0.006***	
	(2.41)	
Log of telephones per people		0.022***
		(3.64)
Ethnic	-0.005	-0.004
	(-0.75)	(-0.54)
No. Obs.	175	179
Adj R2	0,56	0,57

Source: Own Calculations. Note: t-stats in parentheses *0.1, **0.05, ***0.01 Significance level.

Table A.11: Balanced Panel Robustness Check

Dependent Variable: Growth rate 1960-1989				
Variable	1	2	3	4
Dummy for the 1960s	-0.207	-0.212	-0.142	-0.066
	(0.079)***	(0.078)***	(0.074)*	(0.075)
Dummy for the 1970s	-0.205	-0.209	-0.137	-0.063
	(0.079)***	(0.078)***	(0.074)*	(0.075)
Dummy for the 1980s	-0.225	-0.229	-0.154	-0.080
	(0.079)***	(0.078)***	(0.074)**	(0.075)
Dummy for the 1990s	-0.218	-0.222	-0.153	-0.078
	(0.079)***	(0.078)***	(0.074)**	(0.075)
Dummy SSA	-0.013	-0.014	-0.012	-0.013
	(0.004)***	(0.004)***	(0.004)***	(0.004)***
Dummy LA& Caribbean	-0.019	-0.017	-0.013	-0.014
	(0.003)***	(0.003)***	(0.003)***	(0.003)***
Log of initial income	0.063	0.065	0.051	0.038
	(0.020)***	(0.020)***	(0.018)***	(0.018)**
Log of initial income squared	-0.004	-0.004	-0.004	-0.004
	(0.001)***	(0.001)***	(0.001)***	(0.001)***
Log of schooling	0.010	0.009	0.010	0.003
	(0.004)**	(0.004)**	(0.004)**	(0.004)
Assassinations		-24.813	-17.867	-17.254
		(9.871)**	(8.968)**	(8.751)**
Financial Depth			0.017	0.013
			(0.005)***	(0.005)***
Black Market Premium			-0.019	-0.017
			(0.004)***	(0.004)***
Fiscal surplus/GDP			0.122	0.129
			(0.029)***	(0.028)***
Log of telephones per people				0.01
				(0.005)***
Ethnic	-0.018	-0.018	-0.013	-0.009
	(0.006)***	(0.006)***	(0.005)**	(0.005)
No. Obs.	257	257	257	257
Adj R2	0.60	0.61	0.69	0.70

Source: Own Calculations. Note: p-value in parentheses *0.1, **0.05, ***0.01 Significance level.

Appendix B

Table B.1: Characteristics of Householders and Non-Coresiding (NC) Family Members, 1993

	Head/Spouse	Children hh	Children nc	Siblings hh	Siblings nc	Parents hh	Parents nc
Average number per household	1.7	0	0	0	2	0	0,4
Percentage married	88	6	60	8	66	14	.
Percentage not yet married	2	92	38	79	10	1.4	.
Average Age	43	12	12.5	27.5	39	67	38
Percentage with							
primary education	51	42	47	36	41	23	34
secondary education	24	25	36	45	19	2	6
tertiary education	4	2	7	7	3	1	0
Females as a percentage of nc			53		49		46
Percentage out of province			27		17		17
Percentage working	65	8	52	4	58	3	46
Av. working hours per week j1	42	42		49		34	
Av. working hours per week j2	27	18		16		25	

Source: Own Calculations.

Note: Columns 3 to 8 sort the relatives of couples according to place of residence.
nc=non-coresiding, hh=household.

Table B.2: Transfer activities and flows 1993 PPP USD

received and/or given to	All	Children	Siblings	Parents
Percentage of households who:				
receive or give transfers	78	29	50.5	50
receive transfers only	14	11	14	6
both receive and give transfers	39.5	8.5	20	15
give transfers only	25	9	17	29
on balance receive net transfers	20.5	16	22	11
on balance give net transfers	30	13	27	37
on balance receive/give zero				
Transfer flows:				
Mean net transfers received	-252	-38	-46	-145
Mean per capita household income	1206			
Mean per capita household asset value	8063			
Median net transfers received	0	0	0	0
Median per capita household income	361			
Median per capita household asset value	2209			
Net transfers:				
Perc. of hhs with positive net receipts	20.5	16	22	11
Median amount received	99	108	51	69
Mean amount received	805	637	654	593
Median percentage of income	8	11	4	5
Mean percentage of income	19	24	11	12
Perc. receiving less than 10 percent of inc.	32	25	48	47
Perc. receiving more than 50 percent of inc.	20	22	12	13
Perc. of hhs with negative net receipts	30	13	27	37
Median amount given	145	271	63	90
Mean amount given	1141	1341	680	572
Median percentage of income	7	12	3	4
Mean percentage of income	15	21	8	10
Perc. giving less than 10 percent of inc.	39	23	53	51
Perc. giving more than 50 percent of inc.	14	20	9	8
Source: Own calculations				

Note: The category "All" includes all households with non-coresiding children, sibling and parents (relatives of head or spouse). Children, siblings and parents are non-coresiding relatives of head or spouse. The categories "Children", "Siblings" and "Parents" include only those households with children, siblings or parents non-coresiding.

Table B.3: Variable Definitions - Chapter 3

normal hours of work	weekly normal working hours in the past 12 month
number of migrants	Number of household members (children, siblings, parents) living outside couple's household
positive net transfers	ln of positive net transfers per capita, zero if negative or zero net transfers
income	total household income per capita, household level
non-labor income	ln of non-labor income per capita, household level
asset value	ln of asset value per capita, household level
married	Dummy, 0 not married, 1 married
not yet married	Dummy, 0 married, widow/er, divorced, 1 not yet married
secondary education	Dummy, highest level of education attended was secondary schooling
tertiary education	Dummy, highest level of education attended was tertiary schooling
female	Dummy, 0 male, 1 female
age	Age in IFLS3
ill	Dummy, 1 serious health problems in the last 12 month
poor today	Dummy, 1 household indicated to be on the lowest two steps of six-step ladder, 1 poorest - 6 richest
insured	Dummy, 1 head of household/ spouse is holder of heath/labor/private/life insurance
crisis 1998	Dummy, 1 crisis of 1998 had negative consequences for the household
rural	Dummy, 1 rural, 0 urban
government worker	Dummy, 1 if primary employment category was government
private worker	Dummy 1 if primary employment category was formal market
selfemployed with permanent workers	Dummy 1 if primary employment category was selfemployment with permanent workers
selfemployed with temporary workers	Dummy 1 if primary employment category was selfemployment with temporary workers
household shocks:	
death of householder	Dummy, 1 if death of householder occurred in the last 12 month
sickness of householder	Dummy, 1 if sickness of householder occurred in the last 12 month
crop loss	Dummy, 1 if crop loss occurred in the last 12 month
natural disaster	Dummy, 1 if natural disaster affected the household in the last 12 month
business or job loss	Dummy, 1 if business or job loss occurred in the last 12 month
decrease in income	Dummy, 1 if decrease in household income occurred in the last 12 month
cost of shocks	Cost of shock, household level
poor due to no opportunities	Dummy, poor in the village of the household are poor due to no opportunities
number of parents in the hh	
number of children in the hh	
characteristics of hh coresiding	
percentage primary education	percentage of household members with primary education
percentage secondary education children	percentage of household members with secondary education
percentage tertiary education parents	percentage of household members with tertiary education
characteristics of hh non-coresiding	
percentage primary education	percentage of migrants with primary education
percentage secondary education	percentage of migrants with secondary education
percentage tertiary education	percentage of migrants with primary education
percentage out of province	percentage of migrants living out of province where couple's household is located
percentage disabled	percentage of migrants disabled
positive net transfers 1993	ln of positive net transfers survey 1993 per capita
number of migrants 1993	Number of migrant children survey 1993

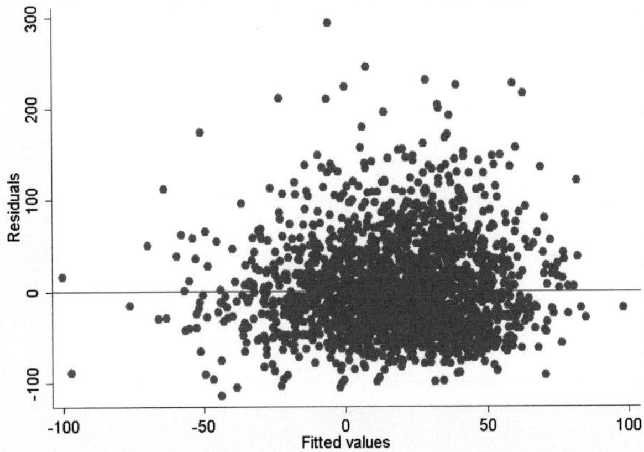

Figure B.1: Residual Plot 1: First Differences - Normal Hours Worked per Week

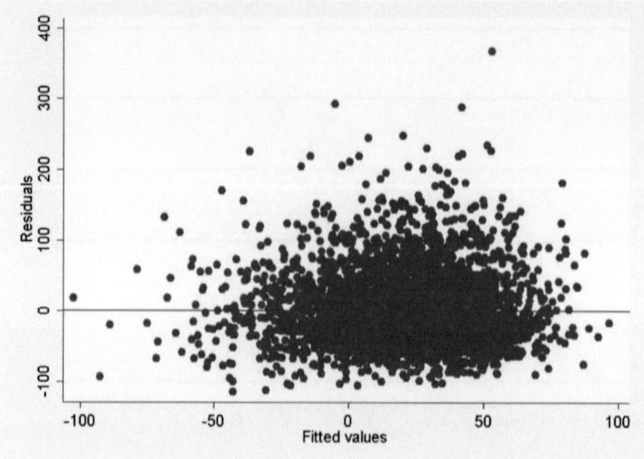

Figure B.2: Residual Plot 2: First Differences - Normal Hours Worked per Week

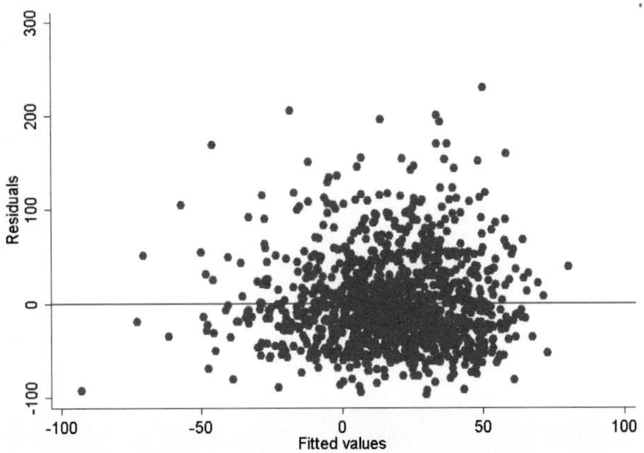

Figure B.3: Residual Plot 3: First Differences - Normal Hours Worked per Week

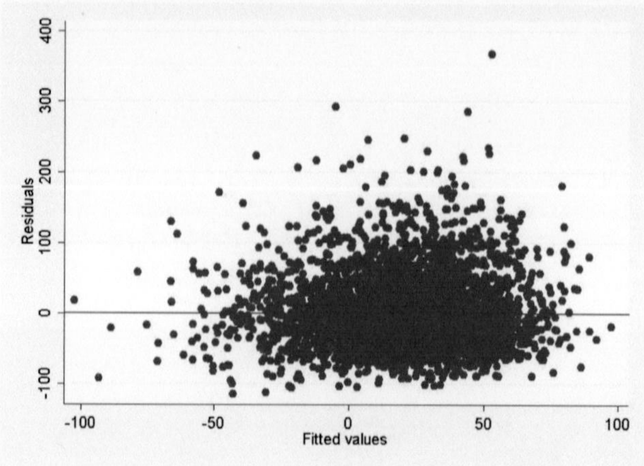

Figure B.4: Residual Plot 4: First Differences - Normal Hours Worked per Week

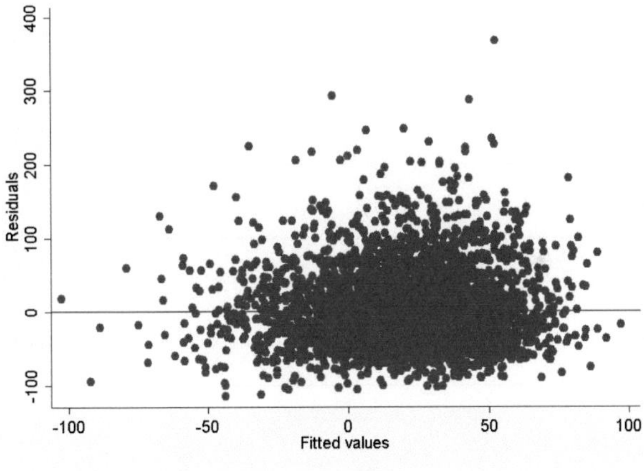

Figure B.5: Residual Plot 5: First Differences - Normal Hours Worked per Week

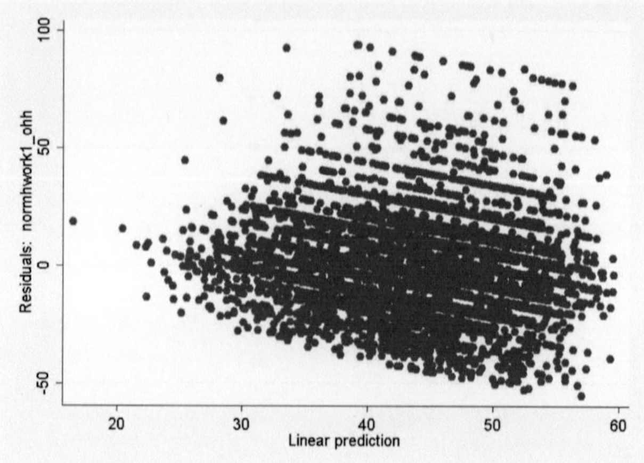

Figure B.6: Residual Plot of the Transfer Regression

Table B.4: Descriptive Statistics of Explanatory Variables - Fixed Effects Model - Household

Variable	Mean	Standard Deviation	Min	Max
rural	0.573	0.495	0	1
ln asset value per capita 1993	13.572	2.159	0	19.70
ln non-labor income per capita 1993	3.573	4.954	0	15.38
age of head in the household 1993	41.365	11.019	17	86
female	0.092	0.288	0	1
opportunities 1993	0.776	0 .417	0	1
shock prior to 1993	0 .036	0.187	0	1
percentage of hh members 1993 with				
primary education	0.202	0.195	0	0.83
secondary education	0.103	0.165	0	0.80
tertiary education	0.006	0.043	0	0.60

Source: Own calculations.

Table B.5: Ordinary Least Squares Regressions

1999/2000	(1)	(2)	(3)
	Migrants	Positive Net Transfers	Working Hours
non-labor income			.0022 (0.04)
asset value		-.2023*** (-4.32)	.2650 (1.43)
household income	.1189*** (4.86)		
married		-1.604*** (-6.08)	1.783 (1.57)
not yet married			-7.970** (-1.83)
secondary education		-.8185*** (-3.92)	-.1216 (-0.16)
tertiary education		-.9438*** (-2.60)	-4.623*** (-3.42)
female			-1.754*** (-2.62)
age	-.0629*** (-15.24)		-.2108*** (-5.80)
ill			-3.414*** (-2.86)
poor today		.4089*** (2.61)	
insured		-.7368*** (-3.36)	
crisis 1998		.0946 (0.58)	
rural			-5.790*** (-8.66)
government worker			-4.578*** (-3.91)
private worker			2.205*** (2.84)
selfemployed with permanent workers			2.308 (1.11)
selfemployed with temporary workers			4.243*** (5.44)
household shocks:			
death of householder		.7837* (1.79)	
sickness of householder		.6677*** (2.33)	
crop loss		.3790 (1.29)	
natural disaster		.1389 (0.17)	
business or job loss		.5599 (1.07)	
decrease in income		.1775 (0.42)	
cost of shocks		0.012 (0.37)	
poor due to no opportunities			-.0397 (-0.06)
number of parents in the hh		-.5197*** (-2.49)	
number of children in the hh		-.0619 (-1.23)	
characteristics of hh coresiding			
percentage primary education			-2.743 (-1.60)
characteristics of hh non-coresiding			
percentage primary education		.5647* (1.69)	
percentage secondary education		1.734*** (4.13)	
percentage tertiary education		3.291*** (4.05)	
percentage out of province		.5706* (1.78)	
percentage disabled		-1.630 (-0.45)	
positive net transfers from siblings 93		.5506*** (8.79)	
number of migrants 1993	.7258*** (87.19)		
Number of observations	5029	5029	5029
Adjusted R-Squared	0,63	0,044	0,058

Source: Own calculations. T-statistic in parenthesis. Note:*0.1, **0.05, ***0.01 Significance level.

Note: Province Dummies were also included in regression 3, but are not reported here. These provinces are North Sumatra, West Sumatra, South Sumatra, Lampung, West Java, Cental Java, Yogyakarta, East Java, Bali, West NusaTenggara, South Kalimantan and South Sulawesi. Left-out province is Jakarta.

Table B.6: Three-Stage Least Squares Regression - Informal Sector: Incentive effect on working hours of head/spouse

1999/2000	(1)	(2)	(3)
	Migrants	Positive Net Transfers	Working Hours
Number of migrants		-0.015 (-0.42)	0.008 (1.81)
positive net transfers			-0.022 (-2.08)
non-labor income			-0.002 (-0.61)
asset value		-0.267 (-4.25)	0.003 (0.44)
household income	0.136(4.29)		
married		-2.298 (-6.35)	0.015 (0.30)
not yet married			-0.168 (-0.82)
secondary education		-0.433 (-1.59)	-0.053 (-1.65)
tertiary education		-0.815 (-1.11)	-0.034 (-0.40)
female			-0.040 (-1.41)
age	-0.065 (-12.24)		-0.006 (-3.58)
ill			-0.063 (-1.34)
poor today		0.321 (1.61)	
insured		0.008 (0.02)	
crisis 1998		0.0477 (0.22)	
rural			-0.143 (-5.04)
selfemployed with temporary workers			0.110 (4.45)
household shocks:			
death of householder		0.810 (1.45)	
sickness of householder		0.729 (1.70)	
crop loss		0.425 (0.78)	
natural disaster		-0.869 (-0.83)	
business or job loss		0.336 (0.40)	
decrease in income		-0.218 (-0.36)	
cost of shocks		0.016 (0.38)	
poor due to no opportunities			0.003 (0.09)
number of parents in the hh		-0.666 (-2.26)	
number of children in the hh		-0.105 (-1.64)	
characteristics of hh coresiding			
percentage primary education			-0.020 (-0.27)
percentage secondary education			0.138 (1.93)
percentage tertiary education			0.143 (0.77)
characteristics of hh non-coresiding			
percentage primary education		0.902 (2.18)	
percentage secondary education		1.962 (3.58)	
percentage tertiary education		5.652 (4.34)	
percentage out of province		0.222 (0.52)	
percentage disabled		1.720 (0.40)	
positive net transfers from siblings 93		0.755 (8.58)	
number of migrants 1993	0.707 (62.97)		
Number of observations	2902		
Source: Own calculations			

T-statistic in parenthesis.

Note: Province Dummies were also included in regression 3, but are not reported here.

Table B.7: Three-Stage Least Squares Regression - Non-Agricultural Sector: Incentive effect on working hours of head/spouse

1999/2000	(1)	(2)	(3)
	Migrants	Positive Net Transfers	Working Hours
Number of migrants		-0.018 (-0.37)	0.002 (0.38)
positive net transfers			-0.042 (-2.56)
non-labor income			0.002 (0.54)
asset value		-0.340 (-4.64)	-0.028 (-2.31)
household income	0.234(4.67)		
married		-1.611 (-3.33)	-0.065 (-1.07)
not yet married			-0.058 (-0.26)
secondary education		-0.700 (-1.92)	-0.049 (-1.22)
tertiary education		-0.689 (-1.25)	-0.174 (-2.85)
female			-0.124 (-3.35)
age	-0.068 (-8.10)		-0.006 (-2.31)
ill			-0.057 (-0.90)
poor today		0.318 (1.14)	
insured		-0.508 (-1.45)	
crisis 1998		0.115 (0.41)	
rural			-0.083 (-2.36)
government worker			-0.007 (-0.13)
private worker			0.137 (3.31)
selfemployed with permanent workers			0.195 (1.91)
selfemployed with temporary workers			0.310 (7.03)
household shocks:			
death of householder		0.764 (1.00)	
sickness of householder		0.224 (0.42)	
crop loss		-0.069 (-0.07)	
natural disaster		1.874 (1.06)	
business or job loss		0.660 (0.63)	
decrease in income		-0.594 (-0.58)	
cost of shocks		0.100 (1.68)	
poor due to no opportunities			-0.066 (-1.76)
number of parents in the hh		-0.689 (-1.25)	
number of children in the hh		0.109 (1.20)	
characteristics of hh coresiding			
percentage primary education			0.034 (0.34)
percentage secondary education			0.145 (1.59)
percentage tertiary education			0.483 (2.83)
characteristics of hh non-coresiding			
percentage primary education		0.694 (1.10)	
percentage secondary education		2.138 (2.82)	
percentage tertiary education		2.494 (2.07)	
percentage out of province		-0.397 (-0.78)	
percentage disabled		8.426 (1.36)	
positive net transfers from siblings 93		0.373 (3.65)	
number of migrants 1993	0.700 (44.89)		
Number of observations	1643		
Source: Own calculations			

T-statistic in parenthesis.

Note: Province Dummies were also included in regression 3, but are not reported here.

Table B.8: Three-Stage Least Squares Regression - Agricultural Sector: Incentive effect on working hours of head/spouse

1999/2000	(1)	(2)	(3)
	Migrants	Positive Net Transfers	Working Hours
Number of migrants		-0.011 (-0.17)	0.006 (0.93)
positive net transfers			-0.001 (-0.08)
non-labor income			-0.004 (-0.87)
asset value		-0.063 (-0.57)	-0.026 (-2.02)
household income	0.085(1.99)		
married		-1.977 (-3.23)	0.061 (0.87)
not yet married			.
secondary education		-1.137 (-2.13)	-0.052 (-1.02)
tertiary education		-1.111 (-0.72)	-0.085 (-0.57)
female			-0.172 (-3.65)
age	-0.043 (-4.43)		-0.003 (-1.07)
ill			-0.105 (-1.49)
poor today		0.472 (1.36)	
insured		-1.020 (-1.41)	
crisis 1998		0.201 (0.53)	
household shocks:			
death of householder		0.143 (0.17)	
sickness of householder		1.009 (1.36)	
crop loss		0.845 (0.94)	
natural disaster		-1.517 (-0.58)	
business or job loss		2.662 (1.51)	
decrease in income		0.055 (0.06)	
cost of shocks		-0.069 (-0.94)	
poor due to no opportunities			-0.028 (-0.65)
number of parents in the hh		-1.067 (-1.82)	
number of children in the hh		-0.317 (-3.03)	
characteristics of hh coresiding			
percentage primary education			-0.120 (-1.26)
percentage secondary education			0.096 (0.87)
percentage tertiary education			-0.900 (-1.73)
characteristics of hh non-coresiding			
percentage primary education		-0.132 (-0.20)	
percentage secondary education		2.007 (1.94)	
percentage tertiary education		-0.364 (-0.13)	
percentage out of province		0.326 (0.42)	
percentage disabled		-10.142 (-1.49)	
positive net transfers from siblings 93		0.823 (4.82)	
number of migrants 1993	0.701 (38.07)		
Number of observations	840		
Source: Own calculations			

T-statistic in parenthesis.

Note: Province Dummies were also included in regression 3, but are not reported here.

Table B.9: Three-Stage Least Squares Regression - Formal Sector: Incentive effect on working hours of head/spouse

1999/2000	(1)	(2)	(3)
	Migrants	Positive Net Transfers	Working Hours
Number of migrants		0.008 (0.22)	0.002 (0.49)
positive net transfers			-0.007 (-0.55)
non-labor income			-0.003 (-1.37)
asset value		-0.111 (-1.59)	-0.004 (-0.58)
household income	0.094(2.44)		
married		-0.899 (-1.82)	-0.038 (-0.78)
not yet married			-0.214 (-1.57)
secondary education		-1.230 (-3.74)	0.017 (0.60)
tertiary education		-1.182 (-2.57)	-0.113 (-2.87)
female			-0.176 (-6.81)
age	-0.062 (-9.27)		-0.005 (-3.60)
ill			-0.098 (-2.22)
poor today		0.588 (2.33)	
insured		-0.642 (-2.35)	
crisis 1998		0.073 (0.29)	
rural			-0.082 (-3.57)
government worker			4.118 (28.43)
private worker			4.216 (30.33)
selfemployed with permanent workers			4.200 (27.88)
selfemployed with temporary workers			.
household shocks:			
death of householder		0.991 (1.35)	
sickness of householder		0.620 (1.29)	
crop loss		0.381 (0.46)	
natural disaster		2.246 (1.47)	
business or job loss		0.687 (0.78)	
decrease in income		1.048 (1.16)	
cost of shocks		-0.004 (-0.07)	
poor due to no opportunities			-0.025 (-0.92)
number of parents in the hh		-0.003 (-0.04)	
number of children in the hh		-0.147 (-0.48)	
characteristics of hh coresiding			
percentage primary education			-0.007 (-0.10)
percentage secondary education			-0.021 (-0.33)
percentage tertiary education			0.235 (1.86)
characteristics of hh non-coresiding			
percentage primary education		-0.092 (-0.16)	
percentage secondary education		0.660 (0.92)	
percentage tertiary education		1.480 (1.35)	
percentage out of province		1.030 (2.17)	
percentage disabled		-7.552 (-1.16)	
positive net transfers from siblings 93		0.373 (4.25)	
number of migrants 1993	0.746 (60.07)		
Number of observations	2122		
Source: Own calculations			
T-statistic in parenthesis.			

Note: Province Dummies were also included in regression 3, but are not reported here.

Appendix C

Table C.1: Descriptive statistics of determinants 1991-1998 - Chapter 4

	1991	1998
Prime-age adults	2.61 (0.04)	3.22 (0.06)
Farm land	7.00 (0.48)	7.27 (0.37)
Land per equivalent adult	1.89 (0.11)	1.91 (0.13)
age of head	45.11 (0.39)	46.29 (0.39)
head completed primary edu	0.04 (0.01)	0.11 (0.01)
head completed higher edu	0.31 (0.01)	0.36 (0.02)
Children 0-4	0.80 (0.02)	0.74 (0.03)
Children 5-14	1.49 (0.04)	1.58 (0.05)
Adults 60 plus	0.31 (0.01)	0.33 (0.02)
Perc. of female prime-age ad.	0.54 (0.01)	0.54 (0.01)
Road dummy	0.81 (0.03)	0.86 (0.03)
Kilometers to next post off./tel.	15.64 (1.13)	17.91 (2.08)
Perc. of hh with migrants per district	0.45 (0.02)	0.48 (0.02)
Population density	0.16 (0.01)	0.14 (0.01)
Dummy forest region	0.53 (0.03)	0.50 (0.04)
Dummy savannah region	0.23 (0.03)	0.30 (0.04)

Source: Own Calculations.

Notes: Mean values, standard deviations in parenthesis.

Bibliography

[1] Abdulai, A., and Huffman, W. "Structural Adjustment and Efficiency of Rice Farmers in Northern Ghana.", In:*Economic Development and Cultural Change*, Vol. 48, No. 3, 503-521, 2000

[2] Acemoglu, D. B., Johnson, S., and Robinson, J.A. "The Colonial Origins of Comparative Development.", In:*The American Economic Review*, Vol. 91, 1369-1401, 2001

[3] Adams, R.H. "Non-agricultural income, inequality, and land in rural Egypt.", In:*Economic Development and Cultural Change*, Vol. 50, No. 2, 339-363, 2002

[4] Ades, A.F. and Glaeser, E.L. "Evidence on Growth, Increasing Returns, and the Extent of the Market.", In:*The Quarterly Journal of Economics*, Vol. 114, No. 3, 1025-1045, 1999

[5] Aghion, P., Alesina, A., and Trebbi, F. "Endogenous Political Institutions.", In:*The Quarterly Journal of Economics*, Vol. 119, Issue 2, 565-612, 2004

[6] Akerlof, G. A. and Kranton, R. E. "Economics and Identity.", In:*The Quarterly Journal of Economics.*, Vol. CXV, Issue 3, 2000

[7] Akyeampong, K. "Whole School Development: Ghana.", 2005 EFA Monitoring Report Commissioned Study, 2004

[8] Alesina, A. and Drazen, A. "Why are Stabilizations delayed?" In: *The Quarterly Journal of Economics*, Vol. 81, No. 5, 1170-1188, 1991

[9] Alesina, A. and Baquir, R. and Easterly, W. "Public Goods and Ethnic Divisions." In: *The Quarterly Journal of Economics*, 1243-1284, November 1999

[10] Alesina, A., Spolaore, E., and Wacziarg, R. "Economic Integration and Political Disintegration." In: *The American Economic Review*, Vol. 90, No. 5, 1276-1295, 2000

[11] Alesina, A., Devleeschauver, A., Easterly, W., Kurlat, S., and Wacziarg, R. "Fractionalization." In: *Journal of Economic Growth*, No. 8, 155-194, 2003

[12] Alesina, A. and Ferrara, E. L. "Ethnic Diversity and Economic Performance." In: *NBER Working Paper Series*, No. 10313, 2004

[13] Andersen, L. and Terjerina, O.J.M. "The Impact of Aid on Recipient Behavior: A Micro-Level Dynamic Analysis of Remittances, Schooling, Work, Consumption, Investment and Social Mobility in Nicaragua.", In: *Development Research Working Paper Series, Institute for Advanced Development Studies, La Paz, Bolivia*, No. 2, 2005

[14] Annett, A. "Social Fractionalisation, political instabilits and the size of government.", In: *The American Economic Review*, Volume 81, Issue 1, 179-190, 1991

[15] Arifianto, A. "The New Indonesian Social Security Law: A blessing or a Curse for Indonesians." In: *ASEAN Economic Bulletin*, Vol. 23, No. 1, 57-74, 2006

[16] Arnott, R. and Stiglitz, J. E. "Moral Hazard and Nonmarket Institutions: Dysfunctional Crowding Out of Peer Monitoring?", In: *the American Economic Review*, Vol. 81, No. 1, 179-190, 1991

[17] Aryeetey, E. "Globalization, Employment and Poverty in Ghana.", *Working Paper, Institute of Statistical, Social and Economic Research, University of Ghana*, 2005

[18] Aryeetey, E., and McKay, A. "Growth with poverty reduction, but increased spatial inequality: Ghana over the 1990s.", In: *M. Grimm, S. Klasen and A. McKay (eds), Determinants of Pro Poor Growth: Analytical Issues and Findings from Country Cases, Palgrave-Macmillan.*, 2007

[19] Azam, J.-P., and Gubert, F. "Those in Kayes. The Impact of remittances on their recipients in Africa." *Document de travail DIAL Paris*, No. 11, 2002

[20] Azam, J.-P., and Gubert, F. "Migrant Remittances and Economic Development in Africa: A Review of Evidence." *Paper prepared for the AERC Plenary Session, Nairobi, Kenya*, 2005

[21] Balisacan, A. "Effects of non-agricultural employment on rural income inequality in developing countries: an investment perspective.", In:*Journal of Agricultural Economics*, Vol.51, No. 2, 266-288, 2000

[22] Banerjee, A. and Newman, A. F. "Information, the Dual Economy and Development.", In:*Review of Economic Studies*, Vol 65, No. 4, 631-653, 1998

[23] Barrett, C.B. "Rural poverty dynamics: Development policy implications.", *Paper prepared for invited presentation at the 25th International Conference of Agricultural Economists, Durban, South Africa.*, 2004

[24] Barrett, C.B., Reardon, T., and Webb, P. "Nonfarm income diversification and household livelihood strategies in rural Africa: concepts, dynamics and policy implications.", In:*Food Policy*, Vol. 26, No. 4, 315-331,2001

[25] Barrett, C.B., Bezuneh, M., and Aboud A. "Income diversification, poverty traps and policy shocks in Cote d'Ivoire and Kenya.", *Working Paper, Department of Applied Economics and Management, Cornell University, Ithaca*, 2000

[26] Barrett, C.B., Bezuneh, M., Clay, D.C., Reardon, T. "Heterogeneous constraints, incentives and income diversification strategies in rural Africa.", *Report to USAID/BASIS CRSP, Cornell University and Michigan State University.*, 2000

[27] Barret, D. B. "Endogenous Political Institutions.", *Christian Encyclopedia. New York: Oxford University Press.*, 1982

[28] Barro, R., and Sala-i-Martin, X. "Economic Growth.", *New York: McGraw-Hill*, 1995

[29] Bates, R. H. "Ethnicity.", *Havard University*, www.cid.havard.edu/cidpeople/bates/Ethnicity_Paper.pdf/, 2005

[30] Bates R.H. "Rural Response to Industrialization: A Study of Village Zambia." *Yale University Press, New Haven and London*, 1976

[31] Bertrand M., Mullainathan S. and Miller D. "Public Policy and Extended Families: Evidence from Pensions in South Africa." In: *The World Bank Economic Review*, Vol. 17, No. 1, 27-50, 2003

[32] Boayke-Yiadom, L., and McKay, A."Rural-Urban Linkages and Welfare: The Case of Remittance Flows in Ghana.", *Working Paper, University of Bath*, 2007

[33] Bogetic, Z. et al. "Ghana's Growth and Poverty Reduction Story: How to accelerate growth and achieve MDGs?.", *Ghana CEM: Meeting and Challenge of Accelerated and Shared Growth, June 18-19, Accra.*, 2007

[34] Borjas, G. "The Economic Benefits from Immigration.", In: *Journal of Economic Perspectives*, Vol. 9, No. 2, 3-22, 1995

[35] Bryceson, D.F. "Multiplex of livelihoods in rural Africa: recasting the terms and conditions of gainful employment.", In: *Journal of Modern African Economies*, Vol. 40, No. 1, 1-28, 2002

[36] Bryceson, D.F. "African rural labour: Income diversification and livelihood approaches: A long term development perspective.", In:*Review of African Political Economy*, Vol. 26, No. 6, 171-189, 1999

[37] Bryceson, D.F., Jamal, V. (eds.) "Farewell to farms: De-agrarianisation and employment in Africa.", *Aldershot: Ashgate.*, 1997

[38] Cameron L. A. and Cobb-Clark D. "Old-Age Support in Developing Countries: Labor Supply, Intergenerational Tranfers and Living Arrangements" In:*IZA Dicussion Paper Series, Institute for the Study of Labor, Bonn*, No. 289, 2001

[39] Cameron L. A. and Cobb-Clark D. "Do Coresidency with and Financial Transfers from Children Reduce the Need for Elderly Parents to Work in Developing Countries?", *Discussion Papers of Centre for Economic Policy Research, Australian National University*, No. 508, 2005

[40] Case A. and Deaton A. "Large Cash Transfers to the Elderly in South Africa." In:*The Economic Journal*, Vol. 108, No. 450, 1330-1361, September 1998

[41] Casella A. and Rauch J. E. "Anonymous Market and Group Ties in International Trade.", In:*NBER Working Paper Series*, No. 6186, 1997

[42] Center for Research on Inequality, Human Security and Ethnicity (CRISE). 2004. About CRISE. http://www.crise.ox.ac.uk/.

[43] Chami, R., Fullenkamp, C., and Jahjah, S. "Are Immigrant Remittance Flows a Source of Capital for Development?" In:*IMF Staff Papers*, Vol. 52, No. 1, 55-80, 2005

[44] Codjoe, S. "Migrant versus indigenous farmers. An analysis of factors affecting agricultural land use in the transitional agro-ecological zone of Ghana, 1984 - 2000.", In:*Geografisk tidsskrift*, Vol. 106, No. 1, 103-114,2006

[45] Collier, P. "The Political Economy of Ethnicity.", 1998, www.worldbank.org/html/rad/abcde/collier.pdf

[46] Collier, P. and Hoeffler, A. "On economic causes of civil war.", In:*Oxford Economic Papers*, Vol. 50, No. 4, 563-573, 1998

[47] Collier, P. and Lal, D. "Why Poor People Get Rich: Kenya 1960-1979." In:*World Development*, Vol. 12, No. 10, 1007-1018, 1984

[48] Collier, P., and Lal, D. "Labour and Poverty in Kenya: 1900-1980." *Clarendon Press, Oxford*, 1986

[49] Corral, L., and Reardon, T. "Rural nonfarm incomes in Nicaragua: patterns, determinants and implications.", In:*World Development*, Vol. 29, No. 3, 427-442,2001

[50] Coulombe, H., and Wodon, Q. "Poverty, Livelihoods, and Access to Basic Services in Ghana: An Overview.", *Ghana CEM: Meeting and Challenge of Accelerated and Shared Growth, June 18-19, Accra.*, 2007

[51] Cox, D., and Jiminez, E. "Achieving Social Objectives through Private Transfers: A Review." In: *The World Bank Research Observer*, Vol. 5 , No. 2 ,205-218,1990

[52] Delgado, C., and Malton, P. "Determinants and effects of income diversification amongst farm households in Burkina Faso.", In: *Journal of Development Studies*, Vol. 28, No. 1, 264-296, 1992

[53] Dercon, S. "Income risk, coping strategies and safety nets.", In: *Wider Discussion Paper Series*, No. 22, 2002

[54] Dercon, S. "Wealth, risk and activity choice: cattle in Western Tanzania.", In: *Journal of Development Economics*, Vol. 55, No. 1, 1-42, 1998

[55] Dercon, S., and Krishnan, P. "Income portfolios in rural Ethiopia and Tanzania: choices and constraints.", In: *Journal of Development Studies*, Vol. 32, No. 6, 850-875, 1996

[56] Desai, M.A., Foley, C.F., and James R.H. "Foreign direct Investment and the Domestic Capital Stock.", In: *The American Economic Review*, Vol. 95, No. 2, 33-38, 2005

[57] Deshingkar, P. and Grimm, S. "Voluntary Internal Migration: An Update.", *Overseas Development Institute, London*, 2004

[58] Deshingkar, P. and Start, D. "Seasonal Migration for Livelihoods in India: Coping, Accumulation and Exclusion.", *Working Paper, Overseas Development Institute, London*, No. 220, 2003

[59] Dickson, E. and Scheve, K. "Social Identity, Political Speech, and Electoral Competition." *Working Paper, www-personal.umich.edu/ scheve/edks0204.pdf*, 2004

[60] Easterly, W. and Levine, R. "Africa's Growth Tragedy: Policies and Ethnic Divisions.", In: *The Quarterly Journal of Economics.*, Vol.112, No. 4, 1203-1250, 1997

[61] Easterly, W. "The Middle Class Consensus and Economic Development.", In: *Journal of Economic Growth*, Vol.6, Issue 4, 317-335, 2001

[62] Easterly, W. "Can Institutions Resolve Ethnic Conflict.", In: *Economic Development and Cultural Change*, Vol. 49, No. 4, 687-706, 2001

[63] Easterly, W. "Empirics of Strategic Interdependence: The Case of the Racial Tipping Point.", In: *DRI Working Paper*, No.5, 2004

[64] Elbers, C., and Lanjouw, P. "Intersectoral transfer, growth and inequality in rural Ecuador.", In: *World Development*, Vol. 29, No. 3, 481-496, 2001

[65] Ellis, F. "The determinants of rural livelihood diversification in developing countries.", In: *Journal of Agricultural Economics*, Vol. 51, No. 2, 289-302, 2000

[66] Ellis, F., and Freeman H.A. "Rural Livelihoods and Poverty Reduction Strategies in Four African Countries.", In: *Journal of Development Studies*, Vol. 40, No. 4, 1-30, 2004

[67] Englebert, P. "Solving the Mystery of the Africa Dummy.2, In: *CEPR Discussion Paper Series*, No. 4616, September 2004

[68] Epstein, G.S., and Gang I. "Ethnic Networks and International Trade.", In: *World Development*, Vol. 28, No. 10, 1821-1835, 2000

[69] Escobal, J. "The determinants of nonfarm income diversification in rural Peru.", In: *World Development*, Vol. 29, No. 3, 497-508, 2001

[70] Fearon, J. D. "Ethnic Structure and Cultural Diversity by Country.", In: *Journal of Economic Growth*, Vol. 8, No. 2, 195-222, 2003

[71] Feldstein, M. "The Effects of Outbound Foreign Direct Investment on the Domestic Capital Stock.", In: *NBER Working Paper Series*, No. 4668, 1994

[72] Ferreira, F.H.G., and Lanjouw, P. "Rural non-agricultural activities and poverty in the Brazilian Northeast.", In: *World Development*, Vol. 29 ,No. 3, 509-528, 2001

[73] Fluitman, F. and Momo J.J.M. "Skills and Work in the Informal Sector: Evidence from Yaoundé, Cameroon.", *Occasional Papers of the International Training Centre of the ILO*, 2001

[74] Francis, E., and Hoddinott, J. "Migration and differentiation in Western Kenya: a tale of two sub-locations.", In: *Journal of Development Studies*, Vol. 30, No. 1, 115-145, 1993

[75] Frankel, J. A., and Romer, D. "Does Trade Cause Growth?", In: *The American Economic Review*, Vol. 89, No. 3, 379-399, 1999

[76] Frankenberg E. and Kuhn R. "The Implications of Family Systems and Economic Context for Intergenerational Transfers in Indonesia and Bangladesh." In: *CCPR Working Paper Series*, No.27, August 2004

[77] Funkhouser E. "Migration from Nicaragua: Some Recent Evidence." In: *World Development*, Vol. 20, No. 8, 1209-1218, 1992

[78] Funkhouser E. "Remittances form International Migration: A Comparison of El Salvador and Nicaragua." In: *The Review of Economics and Statistics*, Vol. 77, No. 1, 137-146, 1995

[79] Gatti, R. "Family Altruism and Incentives." In: *Scandinavian Journal of Economics*, Vol. 107, No. 1, 67-81, 2005

[80] Girma, S., and Yu, Z. "The Link between Immigration and Trade: Evidence from the UK.", In: *GLM Research Paper, University of Nottingham*, No. 23, 2000

[81] Gould, D. M. "Immigrant Links to the Home Country: Empirical Implications for U.S. Bilateral Trade Flows.", In: *The Review of Economics and Statistics*, 302-316,1994

[82] Greenwood, M.J. "Internal Migration in Developed Countries.", In: *Handbook of Population and Development Economics, Volume 1B, Amsterdam: Elsevier*, 1997

[83] Greif, A. "Contract Enforcement and Economic Institutions in Early Trade: The Mehgrebi Traders' Coalition.", In: *The American Economic Review*, Vol. 83, No. 3, 525-548, 1993

[84] Haggblade, S., Hazell, P., and Reardon, T. "The rural non-agricultural economy: pathway out of poverty.", *International Food Policy Research Institute and Michigan State University, Research Workshop 'The Future of Small-Farms', June 26-29, UK*, 2005

[85] Haggblade, S., Hazell, P., and Reardon, T. "Strategies for stimulating poverty-alleviating growth in the rural nonfarm economy in developing countries.", *International Food Policy Research Institute and the Rural Department, World Bank, Washington D.C.*, 2002

[86] Heckman, J.J. "What Has Been Learned About Labor Supply in the Past Twenty Years?" In: *The American Economic Review*, Vol. 83, No. 2, 116-121, 1993

[87] Hugo, G.J. "Asian Experiences in Remittances.", In: *Terry, D.F., and Wilson, S.R. (eds) Beyond Small Change: Making Migrant Remittances Count. Inter-American Development Bank*, 2005

[88] International Labour Office "Employment, incomes and equality: a strategy for increasing productive employment in Kenya.", *Geneva: ILO*, 1972

[89] International Labour Office "The Informal Sector.", *Regional Office for Asia and the Pacific, Geneva: ILO*, 2000

[90] International Monetary Fund "Ghana: Ex-Post Assessment of Longer-Term Program Engagement.", *IMF Country Report*, No. 2111, 2007

[91] International Monetary Fund "Ghana: Selected Issues.", *Staff Country Report* , No. 2, 2000

[92] Islam, N. "The nonfarm sector and rural development.", In:*Food, Agriculture and Environment Discussion Paper, Washington D.C: International Food Policy Research Institute*, No. 22, 1997

[93] Itzigsohn J. "Migrant Remittances, Labor Markets, and Household Strategies: A Comparative Analysis of Low-Income Household Strategies in the Caribbean Basin." In:*Social Forces*, Vol. 74, No. 2, 633-655, December, 1995

[94] Jalan, J., and Ravaillon, M. "Geographic Poverty Traps.", *Discussion Paper, Institute for Economic Development, Boston University*, No. 86, 1998

[95] Janvry, A., and Sadoulet, E. "Income strategies among rural households in Mexico: The role of off-farm activities.", In: *World Development*, Vol. 29, No. 3, 467-480, 2001

[96] Juster, F. T., and Stafford, F.P. "The Allocation of Time: Empirical Findings, Behavioral Models, and Problems of Measurement." In:*Journal of Economic Literature*, Vol. 29, No. 2, 471-522, 1991

[97] Kanbur, R. "Welfare Economics, Political Economy, and Policy Reform in Ghana.", In:*Policy Research Working Paper, Washington D.C.: World Bank*, No. 1381, 1994

[98] Kilic, T., Carletto, G., Davis, C., Zezza, A. "Investing Back Home: Return Migration and Business Ownership in Albania.", *World*

Bank Policy Research Working Paper, Washington D.C.: World Bank, No. 4366, 2007

[99] Klasen, S., and Woolard, I. "Surviving Unemployment without State Support: Unemployment and Household Formation in South Africa.", *CSAE Working Paper Series*, http://www.csae.ox.ac.uk/conferences/2006-EOI-RPI/papers/csae/Klasen-Woolard.pdf, 2005

[100] Lay, J., M'Mukaria, G.M.,and Mahmoud, T.O. "Boda Bodas Rule: Non-agricultural Activities and Their Inequality Implications in Western Kenya.", In:*Kiel Working Papers, Kiel Institute for the World Economy.*, No.1314, 2007

[101] Lanjouw, P."Non-agricultural employment and poverty in rural El Salvador.", In: *World Development*, Vol. 29, No. 3, 529-547, 2001

[102] Lanjouw, P., and Feder, G. "Rural nonfarm activities and rural development: from experience towards strategy.", *Draft paper, Washington D.C.: World Bank*, 2000

[103] Lazear, E.: Globalization and the Market for Team-Mates. In: *The Economic Journal*, Vol. 109, Issue 454, 15-40, 1999

[104] Lerman, R.I., and Yitzhaki, S. "Income inequality by income source: a new approach and application to the United States.", In:*Review of Economics and Statistics*, Vol. 67, 151-156, 1985

[105] Lillard L. and Willis R.J. "Patterns of Intergenerational Tranfers in Southeast Asia." In:*Journal of Marriage and Family*, Vol. 64, 627-641, August 2002

[106] Lucas, R.E.B. "Internal Migration in Developed Countries .", In:*Handbook of Population and Family Economics, Volume 1B, Amsterdam: Elsevier*, 1997

[107] Lucas R.E.B. and Stark O. "Motivations to Remit: Evidence form Botswana." In:*The Journal of Political Economy*, Vol. 93, No. 5, 901-918, 1985

[108] Marenya, P.P., Oluoch-Kosura, W., Place, F., and Barret, C.B. "Education, nonfarm income, and farm investment in land-scarce Western Kenya.", In:*BASIS BRIEF*, No. 14, 2003

[109] McKee D. "A Dynamic Model of Retirement in Indonesia." In:*CCPR Working Paper Series*, No.5, February 2006

[110] McKenzie, D., and Sasin, M.J. "Migration, Remittances, Poverty, and Human Capital: Conceptual and Empirical Challenges.", *World Bank Policy Research Working Paper, Washington D.C.: World Bank*, No. 4272, 2007

[111] Mkandawire, T. "Shifting Commitments and National Cohesion in African Countries.2, In:*Wohlgemuth, L, S. Gibson, S. Klasen, and E. Rothschild (eds.) Common Security and Civil Society in Africa. Uppsala: NAI.*,1998

[112] Montalvo, J.G., and Reynal-Querol, M. "Ethnic Polarization, Potential Conflict, and Civil Wars.", In:*American Economic Review, American Economic Association*, Vol. 95(3), 796-816, 2005.

[113] Münz, R., Straubhaar, T., and Vadean, F., and Vadean, N. "The Costs and Benefits of European Immigration.", *Hamburg Institute of Interntaional Economics Policy Report*, No. 3, 2006

[114] Musiolek, B. "Decent Work in the Informal Sector: CEE and CIS Region.", *ILO working Paper on the Informal Economy*, No.7, 2002

[115] Norman, D.W., Simmons, E.B., and Hays, H.M. "Farming systems in the Nigerian Savannah: research and strategies for development.", *Boulder: Westview Press*, 1982

[116] Organisation for Economic Co-operation and Development "Policy Coherence for Development: Migration and Developing Countries. A Development Centre Perspective", *Paris: OECD*, 2007

[117] Organisation for Economic Co-operation and Development "Migration, Remittances, and Development.", *Paris: OECD*, 2005

[118] Ottaviano, G.I.P., and Peri, G..: Cities and Cultures. In:*Journal of Urban Economics*, Vol. 58, No. 2, 304-337, 2005

[119] Park, C. "Interhousehold Transfers between Relatives in Indonesia: Determinants and Motives." In:*Economic Development and Cultural Change*, Vol. 51, No. 4, 928-944, 2003

[120] Posel, D., Fairburn, J.A., and Lund, F. "Labour Migration and Households: A Reconsideration of the Effects of the Social Pen-

sion on Labour Supply in South Africa." In:*Economic Modelling* , Vol.23, 836-853, January 2006

[121] Posner, D. N. "Measuring Ethnic Fractionalization in Africa.", In:*American Journal of Political Science*, forthcoming

[122] Pritchett, L. "Where Has the Education Gone?", In:*World Bank Policy Research Working Paper Series*, No. 1581, 1999

[123] Rajan, R.G., and Subramanian, A. "What Undermines Aid's Impact on Growth?", *Working Paper, International Monetary Fund*, No.126, 2005

[124] Rauch, J. E. "Business and Social Networks in International Trade.", In:*Journal of Economic Literature*, Vol. 39, No. 4, 1177-1203, 2001

[125] Raut, L., and Tran, L. "Reciprocity with Two-sided Altruism in Intergenerational Transfers: Evidence from Indonesian Family Life Survey Data." *Presented at the Seminar on the Economics of Reciprocity, Gift-giving and Altruism. International Economics Association. University of Hawaii-Manoa.*, 1998

[126] Reardon, T., Stamoulis, K., Cruz, M.E., Balisacan, A., Berdegue, J., and Banks, B. "Rural non-farm income in developing countries.", In:*FAO Agriculture Series, Rome: Food and Agriculture Organization*, No. 31, 1998

[127] Reardon, T. "Using Evidence of Household Income Diversification to Inform Study of the Rural Nonfarm Labor Market in Africa.", In: *World Development*, Vol. 25, No. 5, 735-747, 1997

[128] Reardon, T., and Taylor, J.E. "Agro-climatic shock, income inequality, and poverty: evidence from Burkina Faso.", In: *World Development*, Vol. 24, No. 5, 901-914, 1996

[129] Reardon, T., Crawford, E., and Kelly, V. "Links Between Nonfarm and Income and Farm Investment in African Households: Adding the Capital Value Market Perspective.", In: *American Journal of Agricultural Economics*, Vol. 76, No. 6, 1172-1176, 1994

[130] Rodrik, D. "Where did all the Growth go? External Shocks, Social Conflict, and Growth Collapses.", In: *Journal of Economic Growth*, Vol. 4, Issue 4, 385-412, 1999

[131] Rozelle, S., Taylor, J.E., and DeBrauw, A. "Migration, Remittances, and Agricultural Productivity in China." In: *The American Economic Review*, Vol. 89, No. 2, 287-291, May 1999

[132] Schueler, D. "Incentive Effects of Remittances within the Extended Family: The Case of Indonesia.", *Working Paper, University of Goettingen, Germany*, 2007

[133] Seppala, P. "The politics of economic diversification: reconceptualizing the rural informal sector in South-East Tanzania.", In: *Development and Change*, Vol. 27, No. 3, 557-578, 1996

[134] Smith, A. "An Inquiry into the Nature and Causes of the Wealth of Nations.", http://www.adamsmith.org/smith/won-index.htm776

[135] Sparber, C.: A theory of Racial Diversity, Segregation, and Productivity. In: *Working Paper Colgate University*, 2007

[136] Svensson, J. "Foreign Aid and Rentseeking.", In: *Policy Research Working Paper, Washington D.C.: World Bank.*, No.1880, 1998

[137] Tong, S. Y. "Ethnic Networks in FDI and the Impact of Institutional Development.", In: *Review of Development Economics*, Vol. 9, No. 4, 563-580, 2005

[138] UNDP "Human Development Report 2004: Cultural Liberty in Today's Diverse World.", *New York: Oxford University Press*, 2004

[139] Walz, U. "Migration, Humankapital und Wachstum.", In: *Franz, W., Hesse, H., Ramser, H.J., und Stadler, M. (eds.) Wirtschaftspolitische Herausforderungen an der Jahrtausenwende, Tübingen, Germany: Mohr und Siebeck*, 2001

[140] Wolff, F.C., Spilerman, S., and Attias-Donfut, C. "Transfers from Migrants to Their Children: Evidence that Altruism and Cultural Factors Matter.", In: *The Review of Income and Wealth*, Vol. 53, No. 4, 619-644, 2007

[141] Woodruff, C. "Remittances and Microenterprises in Mexico." In: *Santa Cruz Centre for International Development Working Papers*, August 2001

[142] World Bank "Migration and Remittances Factbook.", *Washington D.C.: World Bank.*, 2007 (1)

[143] World Bank "World Development Report 2008: Agriculture for Development.", *Washington D.C.: World Bank.*, 2007 (2)

[144] World Bank "Global Development Finance: The Development Potential of Surging Captal Flows.", *Washington D.C.: World Bank.*, 2006 (1)

[145] World Bank "Global Economic Prospects 2006.", *Washington D.C.: World Bank.*, 2006 (2)

[146] World Bank "Promoting Improvements in Ghana's Basic Education", World Bank Operations and Evaluation Department, *Washington D.C.: World Bank.*, 2004

[147] World Bank "World Development Report 2003", *Washington D.C.: World Bank.*, 2002

[148] World Bank "The Ghana Governance and Corruption Survey: Evidence from Households, Enterprises and Public Officials.", *Washington D.C.: World Bank.*, 2000

[149] World Bank "Is Growth sustainable? Ghana Country Assistance Review: A Study in Development Effectiveness.", *Washington D.C.: The World Bank.*, 1995

[150] World Bank: World Development Report 1993, *Washington D.C.: World Bank.*, 1992

[151] Yang, D. "International Migration, Human Capital, and Entrepreneurship: Evidence from Philippine Migrants' Exchange Rate Shocks." In: *World Bank Policy Research Working Paper Series, Washington D.C.: World Bank.*, No. 3578, 2005

[152] Yitzhaki, S. "Remittances and inequality.", In: *The Economic Journal*, Vol. 96, No. 3, 722-740, 1982

[153] Zak, P. J., and Knack, S. "Trust and Growth.", In: *The Economic Journal*, Vol.111 , No. 470, 295-321, 2001

[154] Zellner, A., and Theil, H. "Three-Stage Least Squares: Simultaneous Equations." In: *Econometrica*, Vol. 30, No. 1, 54-78, January 1962